Being Prepared

By the same author

Framing Art
Putting a Face on Things
Imaginary Materials: A Seminar with Michael Carter
Fashion Classics from Carlyle to Barthes (2003)
Reframing Art (with Adam Geczy)
Overdressed: Barthes, Darwin and the Clothes that Speak (2013)

Being Prepared: Aspects of Dress and Dressing

Michael Carter

PUNCHER & WATTMANN

First published in 2017

Published by Puncher and Wattmann
PO Box 441
Glebe NSW 2037

http://www.puncherandwattmann.com

puncherandwattmann@bigpond.com

National Library of Australia
Cataloguing-in-Publication entry:

Carter, Michael

Being Prepared: Aspects of Dress and Dressing

ISBN 9781922186942
I. Title.
A821.3

Cover design by Matthew Holt

Printed in Australia by McPhersons Printing group

This project has been assisted by the Australian Government through the Australia Council, its arts funding and advisory body.

Australian Government

Australia Council
for the Arts

As always, for Jenni

Acknowledgements

My thanks to Pru, Karen and Alison for their friendship and conversation; Peter for his kindness; Hilary for her editing; Laleen for her advice; Lisa for her help; Maree for listening; Puncher & Wattman for giving the book a home; Nicholas for the images; Souchou for his encouragement; Joanna for the notebook and Juliet for all the years.

Thanks also to the
Department of Art History and Film Studies,
University of Sydney

A version of ' Superman's Costume' was published in *FORM / WORK* 2000. A version of 'Hats, Ornament and Nature' was published in *Putting a Face on Things*, 1997. A version of 'Blemish Free: Facial Order and the Use of Cosmetics' was published in *Literature and Aesthetics*, 1998.

Contents

1. Superman's Costume   11

2. Hats, Ornament and Nature   33

3. Blemish Free: Facial Order and the Use of Cosmetics   61

4. Why do Stone Age People Wear Furs?   79

5. Formality and Informality in (Mainly) Men's Dress   127

6. Upstairs, Downstairs: The Comings and Goings of Dress   173

Bibliography   205

Dress v. to make ready, prepare.
Dress n. a finish put on something to set off its appearance.
Dressing v. the action of preparing one's appearance.
Dressing n. a piece of material placed directly on to a wound.
Dressed v. having been made ready.
Dressed n. being in a state of readiness.

Chapter One

Superman's Costume

A man had come up along the road on a machine like a small two-wheeled two-seater with its wheels in series, bicycle fashion; lighter and neater it was than any earthly automobile...

H.G. Wells, *Men like Gods*

A multitude of fictional characters have peopled the collective imaginations of the twentieth century. Who, of these characters, is the most famous will always be a matter of dispute — my own candidates for the first half of the century would be Chaplin's tramp and a trouser wearing mouse. The second half of the century is, however, more difficult but there is little doubt that in terms of instant global recognisability the figure of Superman would take some beating. With all of these characters it is their dress that constitutes the most immediate vehicle of their celebrity. What I want to suggest in this essay is that attention to these fictional clothing ensembles can reveal much about the collective imaginative impulses and desires at work in *all* types of dress. In fact one might argue that since these costumes are not required to obey the laws of 'real clothes' it is conceivable that they are more complete embodiments of these imaginative currents than are the actual clothes we wear. It is in this spirit that I want to look at the costume of Superman.

Superman was the creation of Jerry Siegel (writer) and Joe Shuster (artist) and first appeared in June 1938 under the imprint of Action Comics. Over the years the physique of the character has changed considerably but his costume has remained remarkably stable. The red boots and the re-designed chest logo had both appeared by 1940. Whilst not primarily concerned with the narrative dimension of the Superman stories, nor with the nature of the of the comic strip genre in which he first appeared, there are a number of spatial and temporal co-ordinates that must be highlighted if we are to understand the form taken by his costume. Despite a rural upbringing in Smallville at the hands of Jonathan and Martha Kent, most of his exploits as Superman are played out against the skyline of Metropolis. His job as the diffident Clark Kent is in the office of that city's newspaper *The Daily Planet*. It is this access to the flow of information through the newspaper office that enables him to pre-empt criminal conspiracies as well as a succession of natural and human disasters. Superman/Kent replays, in his growing up, the entry of North America into a mature Modernity, a point of development that had the modern city at its heart. He is a modernist hero, familiar with the ways of the city and, paradoxically, dependent upon both the anonymity that it affords and the spectacular setting it provides to pursue his social mission.

Although dwelling on planet earth, he was not born here. In the first frame of the first issue the caption explains his origins.

> As a distant planet was destroyed by old age, a scientist placed his infant son within a hastily devised spaceship, launching it toward earth!

The effect of this double origin is that whilst living in the present as Clark Kent, as Superman he shifts into a 'future-in-the-present'. This unearthly tense, his arrival from the future, is explained so:

> Attendants, unaware the child's physical structure was millions of years advanced of their own, were astounded at his feats of strength.

The geographical distance travelled as a baby is manifested in his earthly life as futurity. Indeed there has been a telling shift in the general alignment of the various futures in play in Superman. At first, the *mise-en-scène* provided by Metropolis appears to be slightly in advance of the time of its readers. At the time of writing this essay (2012) the 'feel' of the character and his world is that of the 'just passed'. The increasing 'humanisation' of the character, particularly in the Lois and Clark TV series, seems to indicate that the modernist co-ordinates of his birth are starting to fade away. The 'amazing powers' that he is capable of, are the legacy of the 'advanced' science and technology of the planet from whence he came, but on earth these 'powers' are compressed into his very physical constitution. Thus, the inhabitants of Metropolis encounter the future by the great man's mere presence. It will be the contention of this essay that the costume of Superman can be understood as an imaginative projection of certain tendencies within Modernity, that is Superman's costume imaginatively 'completes' the male clothing of the modernist metropolis.

The Modernization of the Future

By the time the first issue of Superman appeared in 1938 the imagined future of the West had itself been subjected to an intense process of modernisation. The most immediate manifestation of this was the appearance, in the years after the First World War, of a 'futurist' style of future. In the latter half of the nineteenth century, projections forward in time had been 'modernist' in intent but not futurist in style. The modernist future was, in fact, remarkably plural before its stylistic unification in the nineteen twenties. This plurality was driven by a set of competing social ideologies about the role and place that technological innovation (code name for work) was to have in the future society. A useful distinction with which to make sense of these differing versions of the future is that suggested by Frederic Jameson.(1) He identifies, beyond overt political orientation, two organising principles. The first he calls the, 'technological or organisational' whilst the second he terms the 'libidinal or aesthetic'.

In the former the imaginative space of the future is filled with visions of technological improvement, which in turn are the model for social improvement. Modes of transport get faster, machines gain in efficiency whilst the metabolic flow of the urban masses increases exponentially. In the 'libidinal-aesthetic vision', technology is regarded as a double-edged sword. Tamed and made subordinate to the aesthetic and emotional needs of the whole person, it can be a force for human liberation. However, if it becomes an end in itself, then it will make slaves of us all and we will be remade in the image of the machine. Prior to the First World War one cannot really ascribe any distinct style to either of these tendencies.

Illustration 1. Superman: No.1, 1938 (Superman ™ DC Comics © 1999)

What emerges in the nineteen twenties and thirties is a material analogue to match a future construed as a generalised movement of progressive rationalisation. This style is admirably captured by H.G. Wells in the quotation at the head of this piece. Anything that comes from this future would be 'lighter and neater' than its counterpart in the present. Anything with pretensions to be moving into the future, or desirous of being 'ahead of the pack', would likewise have to exhibit a greater presence of these 'progressive' design characteristics. This comparative moment in which the physical form taken by objects, buildings, cities and people was capable of being read in terms of their material, ethical and even spiritual advancement came to constitute almost the only way in which the future could be thought about and imagined. By the time of Superman's appearance in the late nineteen thirties a very precise futurist style had emerged. It was a visualisation of the future that was able to show the viewer 'progress' enacted right there in the picture. Elements from the imagined future had to be recognised as being the counterparts of contemporary reality, the world of the viewer. Progress was demonstrated by the degree to which the world had travelled along the highway of 'lighter and neater'. This general rule applied to the appearance of the inhabitants of this future world just as much as it did to their material equipment. A version of this is played out in the appearance and adventures of Superman. Against a contemporary urban backdrop the whole order of an extrapolated modernist future is present in the costume and 'amazing powers' of the hero. He too is 'lighter and neater' than the inhabitants of the here and now (see Illustration 1).

The Costume

At the heart of the Superman drama lies the costume change he undergoes when metamorphosing from Clark Kent into Superman (or vice versa). As Clark Kent, the dress he adopts is a version of contemporary male business dress (some deference is paid to his occupation as a journalist along with a degree of North American informality). White shirt, tie, dark blue sports jacket, homburg and dark brown trousers (see Illustration 2). On becoming Superman, he discards these 'street clothes' and assumes them once his 'super' interlude comes to an end. His futurist 'uniform' appears from beneath these contemporary garments and it is this sartorial sequence that suggests a relationship — albeit a hidden one — between his two modes of dress see (see Illustration 3).

Illustration 2. Clark Kent: No.1, 1938
(Superman™ DC Comics © 1999).

Illustration 3. Superman becomes Clark Kent No.1, 1938
(Superman ™ DC Comics © 1999).

In her essay 'Utopian Dress', Aileen Ribeiro has suggested that the sartorial imagination works in a way similar to other forms of the imagination. (2) Nothing gets created *ex nihilo* and in order to conjure up what is 'not yet' the 'has been' gets pressed into service. In the case of Superman's costume a number of elements seem to be drawn from the past, or at least originate out of a vernacular memory of earlier European dress styles. The nature of these 'selections' is by no means arbitrary. The first imperative working on the imaginative ensemble is a negative one in that what Superman wears has to be clearly differentiated from his dress as Clark Kent. Male garments that pre-date modern male bourgeois dress become available for reworking but only if they are also consistent with the 'futurist' style found in the forward projections mentioned earlier. Thus a certain debt may be owed to the form of male costume that emerged in the fifteenth century. For instance, the cloak/cape has the advantage of pre-dating the rise of fitted outer garments as well as being an excellent indicator of physical dynamism. The neck is freed from the collar, tie, and shirt ensemble in favour of a one-piece tunic with a scooped neckline. (3) On the legs are coloured tights that resemble the male hosiery that emerged from under the medieval surcoat. The tight fitting boots have the advantage of solving that awkward matrix of shoes, socks and the trouser cuff.(4) But, as I intimated earlier, the forces shaping the great man's costume are not just negative ones.

Superman is a modernist hero and his appearance embodied a localised version — a sartorial mode if you like — of a much broader modernist aesthetic. We would have little difficulty in recognising this if, instead of being a fictional character, we were looking at an object or a building. By this I mean that his appearance is a complex amalgam of modernist styles and aesthetic dispositions all of which we are perfectly familiar with in the context of 'design'. The most immediate of these is streamlining — the distinction between corporeality and clothing is eliminated in favour of a condition of 'clothed nudity'. Here his 'inner form' has fused with his outer appearance. Nothing, apart from the cloak, is allowed beyond this perfectly engineered surface. Remember he is regularly described in terms of his ability to travel at great speed.

Faster than a speeding bullet! Faster than an express train!

A second factor playing over the costume is that of functionalism. Not the fully articulated aesthetic philosophy of high art and design, instead a vague 'feeling' that certain forms — architectural, sartorial, etc. — were somehow able to achieve increased efficiency by taking on a particular look. A number of elements are combined in Superman's costume to signal this look of functional, and so, formal inevitability. As an ensemble his garments appear as an unchanging suite of highly integrated elements. Put less abstractly, his clothes appear to be the result of conscious design. The garments are colour coordinated and each item seems to be constituted by the position it occupies within the whole outfit rather than being the result of historical accident, irrational fashionability or personal inclination. These features, when combined with the fact that his costume never varies, make it seem to be the result of the operation of reason. (5) The final factor concerns the covert relationship between Superman's costume and the 'civilian' clothes of Clark Kent. The sartorial shift from Kent to Superman also enacts a move from the present into the future. What it presents us with is a sort of abrupt extrapolation of a possible sartorial tendency. We are openly invited to compare the gulf that exists between the two forms of dress and yet, at the same time, we are able to speculate on the possible connections between Clark Kent's 'civilian' dress and his costume as Superman. There is more than a passing similarity between the two outfits. Anne Hollander has described the 'classic modern ideal for the design of (male) clothes' in the following way.

> 'The principles boil down to creating a fluid, multipartite envelope for the body, complementing its shape and movement and establishing a constant visible harmony between the body's structure and that of the clothes without heavily emphasising either one'. (6)

It is only as one arrives at that last caveat 'without heavily emphasising either 'one', together with its parti-colouring, that Superman's costume could be said to depart from this modernist sartorial aesthetic.

Beyond the Suit

With the resurgence in the 1980s of the suit as standard dress for male white–collar workers (and the intensification of its presence in the working dress of professional women.), it is hard to recall that in the nineteen twenties and thirties male clothing, and in particular the suit, was the object of much criticism in progressive political circles. Not to put too fine a point on it, the male suit was regarded as being at the end of its useful life and was routinely compared unfavourably to female dress. (7) Although primarily concerned with the reform of female dress, progressive social movements had, since the 1880s, also toyed with the idea of reforming standard male dress which by then had steadied into the three-piece suit, collar and tie, white linen, hat, socks and shoes or boots.

Illustration 4. Rodchenko in his 'Worker's suit'.
Photograph Mikhail Kaufman, c. 1922.

As the work of Anne Hollander and John Harvey has made clear, the guiding form and principles of this style of dress had been stabilised and generally adopted by the male urban masses well before the rise of a set of self-conscious modernist principles in design and aesthetics. (8) (There is an argument to be made that it was the manufacture and design of men's clothing that constitutes an intimation of what modernity would look like.) The criticisms made of male clothing closely followed the lines of Jameson's earlier distinction. The libidinal-aesthetic rejection of modern male dress as ugly can be traced through the Pre-Raphaelites, the Arts and Crafts Movement and the Male Dress Reform Society of the twenties and thirties. (9) The organisational-functional line of criticism (and there were a multitude of variations) dismissed male dress either for its 'dysfunctionality', its archaic nature, or simply because it was emblematic of bourgeois life. A number of attempts were made to imagine a form of male dress beyond the ubiquitous suit. Whilst I would not claim that either the system of clothing devised by Jaeger in the 1890s, or the Worker's Suit designed by Rodchenko (see Illustration 4) directly influenced the form of Superman's costume the principles embodied in these forms of clothing are remarkably similar to those of our hero. The functionalist sartorial future was before all else 'a system', that is the ensemble appeared to be the result of an effort of total design in which every factor had been weighed and integrated into a functioning whole. (10) Again utility is made to appear as the result of rational thought rather than as the outcome of organic tradition. In both cases the body was encased in an envelope that more closely followed its contours than did the suit. Both Jaeger and Rodchenko's designs abolished the clutter that attended the areas of the male throat and that of the foot, ankle, leg in favour of a buttoned-up, seamless look. It is this sartorial future which appears from beneath the working clothes of Clark Kent.

Vernacular Models

If the formal principles governing Superman's costume belong in the same family as modernist design — sartorial or otherwise — the empirical details of 'influence', that is what actual garments may have been part of the eventual mix is much more scattered and ambiguous. The attempt to imagine a form of fully 'rationalised' male clothing had been a deductive process, especially amongst the aesthetic and political elites of European Modernism. In the popular culture of North America in the nineteen thirties, what finally eventuated as Superman was much more likely to result from a mix of vernacular forms of costume and dress which *intuitively exemplified* many of the principles that were self-consciously formulated in the context of high art and design. I should say that I regard the tabulation of influences ultimately pointless if it is undertaken in the hope of definitively determining why a thing is the way it is. Always there occurs the compression, the moment of fusion whereby the imagination 'dissolves, divides and dissipates' in order to re-form anew. With these limitations in mind I would like to suggest the following strands as possible ingredients for the final form of Superman's costume. The circus and the fairground side-show; the nature of male underwear in the early part of the twentieth century and the male bathing suit, especially its form in the nineteen twenties and thirties.

The Circus and the Fairground

Lift him out of the context of *Metropolis* and the comic strip and Superman is a fairly straightforward amalgam of two figures associated with an earlier form of popular entertainment — the circus trapeze artist and the fairground Hercules. From the former he gets the ability to fly whilst the latter bequeaths him his 'amazing powers'. In each case these earlier characters all had costumes that were similar to that of our hero. The costume of the male trapeze performer appears to have been the invention of a French practitioner, Jules Leotard (1830-1870). It was he who first devised the garment that still carries his name. Strictly speaking the leotard is confined to the upper body and consists of a one-piece garment covering the arms and the torso. As can be seen from Illustration 5, it would be accompanied by tights and pumps giving the performer a skin-tight, integrated look and a surface capable of emblematic decoration. A character midway between the trapeze artist and strong man was the 'human cannon ball'. The costume worn by the late nineteenth century French performer (see Illustration 5) bears an uncanny similarity to that of Superman. The strong man of the fairground booths was traditionally clad in white tights, black boots and brightly coloured trunks. Whilst these antecedents may have provided a vague sartorial repertoire for a whole generation of Superheroes and heroines, the key element absent from these costumes is that of futurity. None of them carry an association of progressive rationalisation. That these elements were capable of such a transposition is clearly visible in Illustration 7 where, with the addition of a headpiece not dissimilar to a flying helmet, the whole ensemble starts to acquire a futuristic significance.

Male Underwear

Remembering that Superman's costume emerges from beneath his street clothes, might it not be too fanciful to suggest that male underwear may have provided one of the models for the final costume? (see Illustration 8.) In fact, the story of men's undergarments at the turn of the century reveals a remarkable synthesis of many of the elements — already discussed. For once, high theory and vernacular reality appear to have replicated one another. (11)

By the end of the nineteenth century certain of the garments worn at fairground shows, and in the boxing ring, had been adapted to the needs of the mainstream male population. John L. Sullivan, a North American boxer was wearing long woollen drawers to keep warm in the severe New England winters. By 1895 these 'Long Johns' had swept all before them and were available through mail order catalogues. (12) A later development saw the drawers fuse with the upper garments to become a one piece known as 'combinations' The British costume historians, C. W. Cunnington and P. Cunnington, observed that:

> This garment (combinations), derived from America, became increasingly popular after the war, so that by 1929 'a more general adoption of the one-piece suit for underwear in place of vest and pants'. (13)

Parallel to the developments happening in North America, Europe was arriving at a similar garment via a grounding in philosophy and social theory. Dr Gustav Jaeger, who was discussed earlier, formulated a rather peculiar vegephobic theory of dress. This became the basis for a total rationalisation of the male wardrobe. Every item of masculine clothing was redesigned, becoming part of an overall, integrated ensemble. As well as his more famous 'Jaeger suits', undergarments and nightwear were included in his vestimentary reconstruction.

As well as the constructivist-like display of their principles of production — clearly delineated seams and functional flaps. These Jaeger garments could also look like a 'stripped down' version of the clothing worn above them. Indeed, in many ways Jaeger combinations are rather too functional. They have a decidedly surgical air and draw attention to those animal orifices and appendages that tie us to, what the Russian artist

Illustration 5. Trapeze artist,
Alfred Cadona, c. 1922.

Illustration 6. Human Cannonball, late nineteenth century.

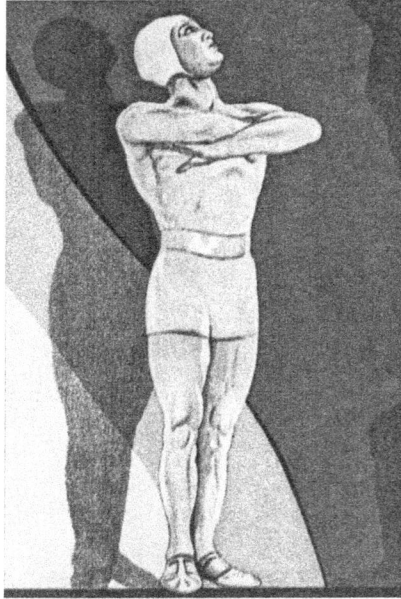

Illustration 7. The Four Kemmys, Circus Act, 1933 (detail).

Illustration 8. Lyle & Scott advertisement, 1950s.

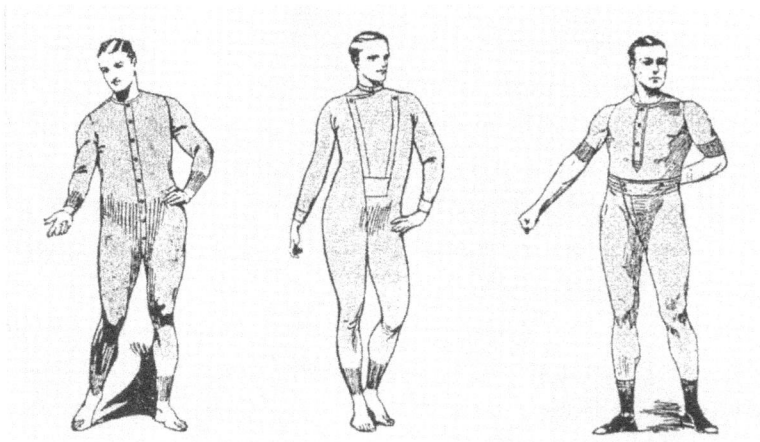

Illustration 9 Jaeger underwear. 1914–15.

Malevich called, the world of 'meat and vegetables'. Thus they conformed to a modernist functionalist aesthetic by appearing to be the essential core of men's outer garments. As the world was purged of its archaic decor by a yearning for progressive rationalisation, the future of male clothes could, so to speak, be glimpsed beneath the rapidly expiring vestiges of the old world in its outer garments.

Swimming and Diving

The character of Superman appeared after the populations of both Europe and North America had been in the grip of an 'aquatic fever' for nearly two decades. The beach and the swimming pool had become one of they key places where a democratic modernity was played out. The cult of sunlight and physical activity, the relaxed mingling of the sexes, modernist swimming pool architecture and the spectacular unveiling of the human body ensured that recreational water and the activities, dress and attitudes that went with it began to acquire a mild futurism. Certainly by the end of the nineteen thirties the denuded human body posed against the clean lines of the new pool architecture had become a favoured site for the fashion photographer. The most recognisable garment worn by our hero is — contrary to the well-known joke about his underpants — a pair of belted swimming trunks. Although somewhat abbreviated than was the current mode, belted swimming trunks were fashionable throughout the nineteen thirties. (14) It was at this time too that manufacturers specialising in swimwear (for example Janzen) began to emerge along with their attendant publicity campaigns. More often than not they used the human figure diving as the most vivid way of showing the new physical pleasures of the pool (see Illustration 10).

Illustration 10. Johnny Weismuller. Florida, 1929.

Flying through air and swimming through water became equivalent activities and so, naturally, required similar outfits.

Conclusion

I have argued that an essential part of superman's costume was its sartorial futurism. It exemplified modernity's dream of going beyond the male suit. Ironically, our hero's only rival was another fictional character who hardly wore anything else — James Bond. He is an alternative modern male hero: part dandy and part action man; solitary, secretive and sexually active, Bond exhibits European irony in the face of American enthusiasm. (15) In the novels (rather than the films) his wardrobe is not that different from that of Clark Kent. Certainly it is worn with a degree of *panache* unthinkable in the bumbling Kent, but nevertheless the suit, that is standard bourgeois male dress, shows no sign of fulfilling the prophecies made for it in the nineteen twenties. As Bond's 'amazing powers' underwent elaboration in the films, his dress remained steadfast. In fact, a favourite ploy of the film character was to reverse the sartorial transformations of Kent / Superman. Bond would be 'hidden' by something such as a frogman's outfit which, when removed, would reveal him dressed in an impeccable evening suit. Beneath the technological outer garments what had been one of the first objects of modernisation was still intact whilst it is Superman's costume that stands revealed as the revolution that never was.

Note and References

(1) Frederic Jameson, 'Introduction / Prospectives to Reconsider the Relationship of Marxism to Utopian Thought', in *Minnesota Review,* No.6, Spring, 1976.
(2) Aileen Ribeiro, 'Utopia Dress', in *Chic Thrills: A Fashion Reader,* eds. Juliet Ash and Elizabeth Wilson, London, 1992. pp. 225-237.
(3) A key area where the future of male costume was fought out was around the neck and throat. Both the aesthetic critique and the functionalist one saw a time when those archaic traces, in the form of the collar and tie, would finally

be swept away.

> 'The time has come when, for instance, the young necks of boys, as well as those of girls, should have their share of light and air not least for the sake of the precious thyroid gland which so largely control, the proper development of body and mind. Unless we give our boys a fair chance, the women of the next generation will surpass the men in a measure that will be of real profit to neither sex nor the population at large.'
>
> *Sunlight*, September 1929, p.31. Quoted in Barbara Burman, 'Better and Brighter Clothes: The Men's Dress Reform Party, 1929 – 1940', in *Journal of Design History*, 8 (4), 1995.

(4) The area around the ankle has always posed a threat to the streamed configurations of sartorial futurism. The sight of another layer (the sock, or the bare ankle) glimpsed through a gap in the magical outer layer seems to be utterly anti-utopian. From Rodchenko's worker's suit, to Superman, to Star Trek, a remarkable consensus has existed on how to overcome this potential embarrassment - tuck the trousers into boots.

(5) Jean Baudrillard elaborates the idea that with the ideology of functionalism, efficiency, reason and progressiveness are signalled not just by unmediated utility, but by 'a look'; an appearance which alludes to an internal integration of the elements within an overarching system. In other words, it not only has to *be* efficient, it has to *look* efficient.

See Jean Baudrillard, 'Design and Environment', in *For a Critique of the Political Economy of the Sign*, St. Louis, 1981.

(6) Anne Hollander, 'Wear and Tear', in *London Review of Books*, Vol.19, No.3, 6 February 1997, p.23.

(7) The psychologist and dress reformer of the nineteen twenties and thirties, J.C. Flugel, remarked so:

> 'We should... endeavour to retain the social advantage at present accruing from the more uniform and sombre male attire without undue sacrifice of the three-fold advantage of feminine dress, i.e. its greater aesthetic value, its greater adaptability to individual needs and taste, and its greater adaptability to changing social ideals. Men's costume needs rescuing from the abject slavery to convention into which it has fallen, a slavery which utterly prevents it from expressing the great changes in outlook and ideals that have taken place since it became stereotyped some sixty or seventy

years ago.'

J.C. Flugel, 'Sex Differences in Dress', in *World League for Sexual Reform: Proceedings*, K. Paul, Trench, Trubner, London, 1930. p.467.

(8) Anne Hollander, *Sex and Suits: the evolution of modern dress*, Kodansha International, New York, 1994 and J.R. Harvey, Men in Black, Reaktion Books, London, 1995.

(9) For accounts of the Male Dress Reform Party see Burman op. cit. and Burman and Leverton, 'The Men's Dress Reform Party 1929-1937', in *Costume*, No. 21, 1987.

(10) For Rodchenko's application of constructivist principles to the design of clothing see *The Future is Our Only Goal: Aleksandr M. Rodchenko, Varvara F. Stepanova*, ed. P. Noever, Prestel, New York, 1991. See esp. p.198 and pp.190-193.

(11) E. Benson and J. Esten, *Unmentionables: A Brief history of Underwear*, New York, Simon and Schuster, 1996.

(12) Shaun Cole, *The Story of Men's Underwear*, New York, Parkstone International, 2010.

(13) C. Willett and Phillis Cunnington, *The History of Underclothes*, London, Michael Joseph, 1951, p.152. The quotation is from a British trade journal, *The Tailor and Cutter*, 1929. The Cunningtons also make the following observation:

> 'All these undergarments, as well as the vest and drawers still worn by many more or less unaltered in design, were very commonly in natural colours. Yet there was a growing taste for something more exhilarating. 'The cult of colour grows apace.' So that there were 'even undervests, drawers, combinations in salmon pink, sky blue, light fawn, peach, etc'.'

Cunnington *ibid*. Quotations from *The Tailor and Cutter* (1929).

(14) For a general history of swimwear during this period see Richard Martin and Harold Koda, *Splash: A History of Swimwear*, New York, Rizzoli, 1990. For a history of swimming see C. Sprawson, *Haunts of the Black Masseur*, London, Vintage, 1993.

(15) See Jay McInerney, et al., *Dressed to Kill: James Bond the Suited Hero*, Paris, Flammarion, 1996.

Chapter Two

Hats, Ornament and Nature

A bonnet is simply an excuse for a feather, a pretext for a spray of flowers, the support for an aigrette, the fastening for a plume of Russian cock's feathers. It is placed on the head, not to protect it, but that it may be seen better. Its great use is to be charming.

Charles Blanc

From the early 1870s through to the start of the First World War, the tops of European women's heads were the scenes of a most extraordinary and bizarre flowering … I refer, of course, to their hats. Once alerted to their presence it becomes difficult to overlook them. At all of the canonical sites of modernity — the street, the cafe, the brothel and the racetrack — there they are, soaring above the assembled throng (see illustration1). Magnificent, but so different to the streamed configurations that were to come. So what was it that underlay the extraordinary events happening on these hats, hats that, at the height of their elaboration, could have circumferences of six feet (1.8m). Why was it that something that was such a ubiquitous witness to the birth of European modernity was totally swept away?

That something rather odd was taking place on the heads of European women from the last quarter of the nineteenth century until the outbreak of World War I has been regularly remarked upon by historians of fashion. Fiona Clark positions the onset of these excessive styles in the 1870s. (1) But it was during the 1880s and the 1890s that this weird aerial pastoral reached a climax, so much so, that Clark characterises the hats of the 1880s as exhibiting an 'unconscious surrealism', while those of the 1890s

Illustration.1 Jacques Henri Lartigue, Maurice Farman in his Biplane, Le Buc, November 1911.

were distinguished by a 'cultivated strangeness'. (2) We can gain some flavour of their peculiarity from the following description:

Millinery (in the 1880's) took a similarly realistic turn and began to emphasise the rank and decaying aspects of nature. Worm eaten autumn leaves, faded field flowers were all recommended … by the end of the decade real twigs, grasses and mosses featured on hats. (3)

Alison Gernsheim also remarks upon the bizarre turn taken by women's millinery at this time:

In the summer of 1887, bizarre Paris hat trimmings included carrots, turnips and beetroot, as well as slightly more orthodox plums, peas, and peaches, besides stuffed birds – whole parrots, love birds, finches, blackbirds and pigeons. (4)

Briggs mentions that in the 1870s women's hats utilised 'birds' heads and even whole birds' (5) whilst Corfield talks of these hats as 'elaborate confections'. (6) Haynes recounts the anecdote of a Dr Bowdler Sharpe, head of Ornithological Department of the Natural History Museum who, during a visit to Paris in 1900, had noted that the milliners' shops were 'full of hats on which were barn owls dyed pink'. (7) By the arrival of the Edwardian era this dense and complex flora and fauna, more like 'miniature habitat groups' than hat decorations, began to dissipate and change. (8)

There was a sudden increase in hat size, allowing a spatial dimension to enter these gardens causing them to distend in some remarkable ways. James Laver, with his usual eye for fashion's strangeness, remarks: 'It was in 1911 that the hat assumed its most startling dimensions'. (9) Fiona Clark and Turner Wilcox note that Edwardian hats attained their maximum width in 1911 'when wide brimmed hats … reached in extreme cases a circumference of two yards (1.8m).' (10) If these hats were little theatres of ornament, what was the drama being played out up there and why such an excess of decoration on the eve of their death at the hands of modernisation? To understand what is happening on the hats we must first have some grasp of what is meant by ornament and decoration in general. Experts on 19th century European female hats are able to date them with remarkable accuracy by using the style of their ornamentation. (Trimmings) This would suggest that the arrangement of these decorations was not an arbitrary one but was more likely to result from the presence of collective aesthetic impulses — something akin to an unconscious of the hand. The following two sections are descriptive explorations of what ornament consists of, while the final section brings together the formal, aesthetic properties of the hats and the historical context in which they occurred.

Ornament and Decoration

The connotations clustering around the word ornament — mantelpieces, knick-knacks, objects vanishing beneath a set of gross decorative mutilations — all speak of something whose golden age has long passed. Ornament was banished from the intellectual canon at the same time it was expelled from the repertoire of aesthetic practice by the rise of modernist functionalism. But it would be hard to find any other term whose fate so closely matches the historical ebbs and flows of the past one hundred and fifty years. Down, but never fully out, ornament has survived the upheaval of modernism only to land back on our doorsteps, but now cleansed of its role as the bad object of modernism. The disappearance of a coherent theoretical accompaniment to a dwindling ornamental practice means that now it can only be approached tangentially. One is forced to reach for the dictionary and the thesaurus in order to trace the affiliations that radiate out from ornament and its synonyms.

The thesaurus reveals ornament to be just one of a family of words that, together, form a complex semantic field. Four verbs are synonyms for one another — ornament, embellish, decorate and adorn. The dictionary fleshes out this quartet in the following way:

> Ornament: quality or person whose existence or presence confers grace or honour; adorning, being adorned, embellishment, features or work added for decorative purposes. (*Oxford Concise English Dictionary* 7th edn, 1982.)

Like so many of these dictionary hunts, the searcher rapidly descends into a labyrinth of referential circularity.

> Adorn: add beauty or lustre; furnish with ornaments.
> Embellish: beautify, adorn, heighten (narrative) with fictitious additions

Decorate: furnish with adornments
(*Oxford Concise English Dictionary*)

Despite the circularity of these definitions it is possible to discern a common thread running through each of these verbs. Ornament, decorate, adorn and embellish all contain the suggestion that an addition of some kind is taking place. In each of these words there is the assumption that an earlier object or situation is altered by something (the ornamental element) being added, or done, to it. However, this earlier object or situation is regarded in itself as being complete, with the four key terms making their additions beneath an aesthetic imperative; that is, they are added in order 'to beautify' the original situation or thing.

To sum up, we find that the four synonyms assume the existence of a complete and independent initial condition of either a thing or situation; there follows the addition of a second register to this initial condition; a relation of priority and rank adheres between these two registers with ornamenting, etc, 'coming after' the thing that is being ornamented; finally the additions are made in order to create a more aesthetically intense state.

This type of relationship is just one of a family of such connections that Jacques Derrida has undertaken to explore with his notion of the supplement. Derrida has identified two types of supplemental relation. The first is a relation that adds something in the sense of making up for a lack in the initial condition. The second adds something extra, something not regarded as integral to the initial concept, situation, or thing. Clearly it is this second form that we are exploring in this context. Ornaments, adornments and decorations, while welcome additions, are not regarded as being intrinsic to the thing in question, rather they are additions deriving from a desire to dress the object, to make it decent and therefore more pleasing. At this level, Derrida's notion of the supplement does little more than provide confirmation for the dictionary exercise. But as deployed by

Derrida, the idea of the supplement drives much deeper into the nature of the relationship between the two registers of the 'object embellished'. In his essay 'The Parergon' he submits a paragraph taken from Kant's *Critique of Judgement* to one of his inimitable readings. It is worth reproducing the paragraph from Kant in full since it deals with, and bears directly upon, the position occupied by ornament.

> Even what is called *ornamentation* (*parerga*), i.e. what is only adjunct, not an intrinsic constituent in the complete representation of the object, in augmenting the delight of taste does so only by means of its form. Thus it is with the frames of pictures or the drapery on statues or the colonnades of palaces. But if the ornamentation does not itself enter into the composition of the beautiful form — if it is introduced like a gold frame merely to win approval for the picture by means of its charm — it is then called *finery* and takes away from the genuine beauty. (11)

What emerges from Derrida's reading of this quotation is that ornament (and its synonyms) is just part of a much broader supplemental field, one that divides the work of art (here used in the sense of artefact) into two registers; the *ergon*, that is the work in essence, and the *parergon*, that is the 'supplemental' additions to the work such as the frame, or ornamentation. The two registers and their relationships constitute a crucial means by which Western aesthetics was able to determine the essential and the non-essential dimensions of any work. It sets in place what can be thought of as intrinsic to the artefact and what should be placed outside in the realm of non-essentiality. The existence of a supplemental relationship on our hats means that there is an essential core to the hat 'proper' upon which is placed collections of decorative motifs, or trimmings. Part of the hat (no matter how diminished) will be devoted to the *ergon* that is to the hat part of the hat. The second register, the *parergon*, is the place where the ornamental unfolds and where a radically different set of imperatives to that of the hat's essential core are in play.

If we return to the thesaurus for one last time, a final strand of meaning remains to be drawn out. As we have already seen, the four key words grouped beneath the heading of ornament stand in a quasi-parasitic relationship towards the intrinsic dimension of the object. The ornamental, by definition, requires a host object in order to make an appearance. Of the four terms — ornament, adornment, embellishment and decoration — it is ornament that signifies the most substantial of the modalities taken up by each of the four supplements. It suggests a certain degree of permanent embedding in its host. Decorate, adorn and embellish imply lesser degrees of physical integration. Here things are hung onto other objects for 'special occasions', but are capable of being easily detached from the host when the occasion is over. In this latter series there is no implication that physical damage would ensue with the removal of, say, decoration. (Note — Many of the trimmings for these hats were detachable. Their wearers would often vary their selection with each 'outing') However, when we examine the adjectival form of ornament – the ornate – a rather more active relationship between the two registers of the object starts to appear. Rather than being a simple addition of something to an already integral, completed object, the ornate hints at the presence of an active transformation of the host object, such that its status as host almost wholly disappears. (Note — the functional part of the hats, such as protection, almost completely disappeared and instead became simply a support for the ornamental events taking place on these stage sets.) We no longer seem to be strictly within the Derridean notion of the supplement. Rather than addition, we have a wholesale shifting of an object from one register to another. We must be precise here. There are a wealth of terms that denote these sorts of transformational shift. Along with ornate we could also include 'distort', 'exaggerate', 'stylise', 'caricature', and 'simplify'. However, the observer of such transformations finds themselves placed in a very precise situation, a situation where they are perpetually recognising the presence of like-in-unlike. Confronted by the ornate, we witness not just the ornamental, but also the process of ornamentation itself. Ornament and the ornamental therefore should not be thought of as simply the addition of a definable set of elements to an essential host object, but as a transformation in which the observer is constantly being moved across the two registers of ergon and parergon. More precisely, we might say that the observer is positioned within the very process itself so that he, or she, is constantly witnessing the one being transformed into the other.

Up to this point we have been looking at the relational element of ornament and its synonyms. But when we resort to terms such as 'ornamental', ' ornate', 'decorative', and so on, we are also calling up, in however vague a manner, some kind of content. To do justice to the complexity of a word like 'ornament', these two aspects, that of a certain type of relationality and that of a specific type of content, need to be held together. Certain dangers are attendant if these two dimensions are treated independently of one another, or if one is emphasised at the expense of the other. For instance, if the relational element alone is stressed, the particularities of the ornamental (the content) vanish into a great ocean of formal similarity. On the other hand, if the ornamental is seen as involving nothing more than content, then a pathway opens up to the compilation of dictionaries of ornament, so popular in Victorian times. The problem with this kind of approach is that the fundamental 'work' of the supplement goes unrecognised. One way leads to purely formalised abstraction, the other to empiricist description.

Theorisations of ornament were relatively slow in throwing off nineteenth-century historicism. Ernst Gombrich captures the essence of these historicist-based formulations so:

> From the observation that decorative motifs can have symbolic meaning,
> it was only too tempting a step to conclude that all motifs were originally

conceived as symbols — though their meaning has been lost in the course of history. If that conclusion was justified a rich harvest beckoned to the historian who deciphered the symbolism of far distant ages. Once the meaning of these designs was established the monuments would again speak to us. (13)

The ornamental was construed as an ensemble of singular, discrete motifs. Each motif was considered to have been explained when both an origin and a primal meaning were 'discovered'. The crucial shift occurred when the ornamental started to be thought of as a system, that is when it began to be conceived of as a structured field of internal dependencies. At this point ornament ceased to be thought of as a collection of individual motifs, each with its own distinct historical pedigree, and came to be seen more as a systematic phenomenon grounded in the operations of a logical order of internal relationships.

While this change of paradigm profoundly altered the way in which the singular ornamental utterance was seen, it was (and still is) the case that this remained embedded within those general semantic networks we have described as being 'a certain relationship to'. The overall meaning of ornament was still to be found in the comparative mood. Perhaps the most frequent theory advanced to explain ornament-in-general was that it constituted a world whose representational order diverged radically from that of the mimetic-perspectival system. Despite considerable divergence over matters of detail, ornament is still positioned as the polar opposite of a pictorial regime whose aim is to produce an accurate copy of the world. The ornamental becomes a system of *representation* that does not have the accurate copy as its chief aim and instead follows a different set of imperatives. The relational element of the ornamental is retained in that the two visual orders are conceived of as consisting of one order that is placed before that of the decorative and which the latter re-works, re-plays, or transforms in some way. That re-working of a 'before' by an 'after', and, therefore, the necessity for there to be a space between the two moments, is described variously by the use of stylisation, simplification, distortion, etc. Whichever formulation is chosen, both contain an element of comparison. It is not my intention to demolish or forswear use of this comparative structure but rather to bring out a number of shortcomings that such theorisations display when they are inserted into a three-dimensional space such as that found on hats, rather than the two-dimensional space which is their assumed dwelling place.

Ornamental Space

If we were to take an aerial view of the hats, it would soon be evident that their distinctiveness did not just derive from the presence of a certain number of motifs. The distribution of these trimmings across the hat's surface — in other words the patterns formed by their spatial distribution — also contribute to their distinctiveness. But just what kind of space is it that lies within these peculiar worlds of hat ornament?

In 1880, Gottfried Semper, in a lecture he delivered on textile design, made the following observation:

> We stand in no need of perspective nor of light and shade, but very much of regular composition. Wherever there are figures in the design they must be shown as much as possible in profile, since profile results much more in the impression of a flat plane than a frontal view. (14)

Most of the themes I want to elaborate upon are present in this quotation. Semper begins by straight away establishing a comparative mood. Not the relay of a three-dimensional reality onto a two-dimensional surface with the aim of producing a virtual three-dimensional illusion, but rather an immediate insistence upon the dominance of the two-dimensional. There is to be no depth in the European sense, that is, no modelling through chiaroscuro, no perspectival recession, simply the arena of flat patterning, or what Semper refers to as 'regular composition'. If there are to be any figurative elements, they are to be rendered, not according to the demands of perspectival recession, not as corporeal objects located within a common set of spatial co-ordinates, but rather according to the demands of composition and two-dimensional space. It is profile or, more accurately, line inscribed upon a surface that is abstracted as the most pertinent feature of the representational matrix, rather than full corporeality. If we were to imagine Semper's ideal, what we would see would be a scene, or rather a pattern, where the distance between figure and ground had become greatly compressed. A more modern characterisation of the ornamental is that advanced by Henri Focillon. (15) The strength of his theorisation of the ornamental rests in the way he is able to keep the aspects of relationality and content in touch with one another. His broad thesis is that artistic styles can only be fully appreciated by paying attention to their distinctive formal transformations. This he characterises as a field of internal dynamics and what later thinkers would call 'formal operations', or 'endogenous relations'. (16) In Focillon, the comparative elements occur in the distance that exists between the inception of a style and its subsequent unfolding. The interval/ space is that moment when the logic of the internal relations of ornament begins to assert itself. Although Focillon describes this process in the language of evolution, the implication is, I think, more modern. At a certain point an earlier stylistic condition crosses into a systematising region. It becomes a visual field which is no longer guaranteed by an external referent of any kind. Instead, the field begins to organise itself in terms of a set of internal apprehensions. There is an order, but this order is now one that derives from the logic of ornamentality. Once the ensemble of representations, motifs, elements and lines crosses this threshold, there is no longer any external 'point' to the field. It ceases to obey the laws of representation and geometry, along with the demand that the shortest distance between two points is a straight line. Instead, it starts to wander. This 'pointless' meandering is not, however, arbitrary, random, or spontaneous; its movements are organised and directed by the logic of ornament. Having established the systematic nature of the ornamental, Focillon shifts his focus to a consideration of ornament's content.

The field of the ornamental is opened by a transformatory act involving the reduction and simplification of an original of some kind. There is some ambiguity in Focillon's account as to whether this reduction and simplification is effected upon the fullness of a previous scene or motif, or whether reduction happens when a degree of etiolation of a scene or motif has already occurred. Either way, it is the process of reduction that is the crucial moment in all of these instances. What Focillon means by 'reduction' needs to be further specified. Reduction is always a more complex process than simply the elimination of elements and their subsequent schematisation. It always involves the rendering of the original into an ensemble of comparable units that then become available for manipulation according to the internal rules of the system. In fact, systematisation in this sense is not reduction at all, but rather a conversion of the original into a field of equivalent units. Over time we can observe a series of driftings that move further and further away from the primal scene or original motif. Focillon now begins to attempt an explanation of the content of the ornamental in the light of these preliminary groundings

.Once the threshold into the ornamental is crossed, the internal dynamic of the forms moves along two different pathways. The first route leads to a geometrical intensification whilst the other opens out onto sinuous elaboration. The primary scene, or motif, disappears into a formal order. This journey is often described in psychoanalytical terms characterised either as a shift away from the mimetic, that is as a move away from the realm of the superego to that of the libidinal, or from the waking

44

world to the world of the dream. Focillon always stresses the immensity of the distance travelled between the two registers. It is a journey from the world of the real and its representation into a realm of the imaginary and the obscure. Focillon describes this new world thus:

> This strange realm of ornament (the chosen home of metamorphoses) has given birth to an entire flora and fauna of hybrids that are subject to the laws of a world distinctly not our own. (17)

For Focillon — and the present author too — the journey entails a move into another realm, governed neither by the need to transmit accurate information, nor by a need to generate accurate depictions of the real world. Focillon's analysis of the ornamental deposits us at the very doorstep of our hats and only falters, in terms of the project under way here, when he starts to explore the relations between the ornamental and space. Once more, we find ourselves up against that dominance of line that we saw at work in Semper. About these crucial relations, Focillon says:

> Even before it becomes formal rhythm and combination, the simplest ornamental theme, such as a curve or *rinceau* whose flexions betoken all manner of future symmetries, alternating movements, divisions and returns, has already given accent to the void in which it occurs and has conferred on it a new and original existence. Even if reduced merely to a slender and sinuous line, it is already a frontier, a highway. Ornament shapes, straightens and stabilises the bare and cold field on which it is inscribed. Not only does it exist in and of itself, *but it also shapes its own environment* — to which it imparts a form. If we follow the metamorphoses of this form, if we will study not merely its armature, but everything else that it may include within its own particular framework, we will then see before us an entire universe that is partitioned off into an infinite variety of blocks of space. The background will sometimes remain generously visible, and the ornaments will be disposed in straight rows or quincunxes; sometimes, however, the ornament will multiply and prolixity and wholly devour the background against which it is placed. (18) (My italics)

This is such a remarkable piece of writing that I make no apologies for quoting its author at such length. What he is doing here is bolting ornament and space together and the meta-category — the active principle — he uses is that of line. If we are to use his complex formulation of ornamental space on the hats, the three aesthetic elements of line, space and ornament need to be disengaged and considered in relation to one another.

The initial construal of ornament in the above quotation rests on the dominance of line. But if we ask 'Upon what, and where, are these lines appearing?' or 'what is it that is making these lines appear and then to move?' then we discover that three more fundamental elements have to be present. Firstly, there must be some material, or surface, upon which the line can be inscribed. There must be a tool of inscription, a stylus. Finally, there has to be a hand, or impetus of some kind, propelling the stylus. (This inscription of a mark upon a surface is, in Focillon's characterisation of it, the movement of line-upon-background, or of figure on ground. By making space subservient to the movement of line, Focillon, despite his profound grasp of the nature of ornament, still remains within the horizons established by Semper. As line traces out the lineament of this 'partitioned off' universe, the object that is continually called up in the imagination is that of a frieze.

Focillon's analysis has infinitely more potential for opening up three-dimensional ornament when he discusses the spatial possibilities that are generated and disseminated by the movement of line. Even though he remains locked upon a two-dimensional surface, the line he tries to capture in its movement is one that has launched itself into a void. As it moves it is capable of soliciting from space a number of latent dimensions. An infinitely variable three-dimensional envelope is precipitated as this line traces a trajectory across the void. A spatial field opens up, but this is not a space held in place by the geometric coordinates of 'our' world; rather, it is something subject to tension, compression and expansion.

It is also a space that can be cut, spliced and stretched according to the requirements of pattern. What emerges is a spatial field that is capable of being flexed in a multiplicity of ways and which is neither, regular, homogeneous or unified.

However rich this conception of ornamental space might be I would still claim that it fails to make a full journey into a genuine three-dimensionality. Even when we take into account Focillon's general typology there is still a feeling that, at bottom, the objects he has in mind consist of two-dimensional surfaces upon which a line has been inscribed. At this point it is worth recalling how he characterised the two potential pathways for ornament to journey down. On the one hand, there were those systems favouring series characterised by a geometric and repetitive progression across a surface. On the other hand, there is the labyrinthine; systems favouring the curvilinear interlacing of a line with no beginning or end. But if we enquire as to the nature of the 'backing' upon which these systems are etched, then we cannot help but feel that it is a flat, unmarked surface, readied for attachment to something else or that the ornamental unfolds within a specific area 'let into' the surface of some more profound object. Even when there is an absence of direct physical attachment — where we have the fully independent, three-dimensional ornamental object — merely having the inscribed surface rotate around its vertical axis reproduces the frieze effect. Simply extending the characteristics of two-dimensional ornamentation into three dimensions is not sufficient to comprehend what is happening on the hats.

The ornamental profusion found on the hats presents these theorisations of ornament with a number of difficulties. The most obvious one is the way in which hats violate the assumption of two-dimensionality and the dominance of line. When confronted with a hat, particularly the ones under review here, it is impossible to recreate the whole from a fragment; or, to put it another way, a single view is not a reliable guide as to what we cannot see. The type of ornament used on hats, in other words the 'frieze effect', is almost completely absent. There is a surface to which trimmings are attached, but this surface approximates more to a platform, or a stage, than to a core or vertical axis. The backing or support for the ornamental order of hats is more like a horizontal plane upon which are stacked a number of elements. In this ornamental order, pattern is weak, repetition unusual, and symmetry absent; and the reason for this is that the spatial configurations within which the ornamental ensembles congregate are not those of figure-ground, nor those in which line is dominant. And yet neither are they arbitrary agglomerations of parts. There is an order of sorts at work in these dream pile-ups. (illustration 2)

Even a cursory glance at these confections will reveal both regularities of form and a common lexicon of units. For instance, there is a repertoire of formalised elements available for endless re-combinations, such as bows, fan-like shapes, generic flower forms, and feathers. Present is what we might call a 'principle of dismemberment', where parts are taken from a whole and inserted into a different totality, like shaping feathers into non-avian forms. The opposite of this can take place, so that parts are reassembled to form new wholes, for instance, parts of flowers might be reworked into alternative organic morphologies such as butterflies. Overall, there is a tendency for these ornaments to favour elaborative extension rather than confinement within strict geometricisation. But such features are only possible because there is an overall subservience to a form of spatiality that is radically different to the one articulated by Focillon. There, it will be recalled, line 'gives accent to the void in which it occurs', but in the sort of space favoured by hat ornament, the exact opposite of this is happening; it is space that is giving accent to the line. In these systems it is space that precedes line since line is generally absent from these hat trimmings. The ornamentation on hats, and the spatial fields they rest in, has something akin to flower arranging, something in common with cake decoration (they are, after all, described as confections), and in some ways similar to jewellery.

How then to think their space? They certainly live and die within a three-dimensional framework, but it is not the three-dimensions of the cube where each side of the cube provides a surface upon which can be inscribed the ornamental elements, rather we might characterise it as a three-dimensional envelope of surprising plasticity. This envelope could be compressed so that a great deal can happen in a restricted volume. It can also expand, enlarge and stretch outwards from the wearer's head, so that an area of compression, in which we may discover the flora and fauna of schematised woodland, can be found next to a space that leaps out into the void, tracing out the line with a feather. Space up here is multiple, curved and subject to a bewildering succession of miniaturisations and distensions. What we find in the ornamental order of hats is a world where space itself is artificial and unreal. We must now turn to the question of what is to be found in such peculiar environments.

The Last Ornament

No matter how varied the range of motifs become, one thing remains constant. All the trimmings derive in some way or other from nature. To the best of my knowledge hats have never been trimmed with, say, household cutlery or mechanical parts. The question is if nature is such a central part of hat decoration, what sort of nature is it and what is it doing on the platforms provided by these hats?

Discussing the effects of modernist functionalism upon the equipment of daily life, Susan Buck-Morss comments that:

> Functionalism stripped technology of its casings. In women's fashions as well, the casings of corsets, crinolines, and long skirts disappeared. In

Illustration 2: Jacques Henri Lartigue:
The Races at Auteuil: 1911

hairstyles and office buildings, the demolition of nineteenth-century styles left no area of daily life untouched. (19)

She continues:

> Nineteenth century design may have been technologically reactionary when it hid function and tried to revive dying forms, but the tremendous value of its clutter was that it tacked onto the surface of things all kinds of configurations in which historical truths and utopian dreams could be read. (20)

Thus it was that the whole order of the ornamental was shunted into the past to become the 'bad object' of the new. Buck-Morss' observation regarding this 'last' moment of European ornament opens up the hats to the thought of Walter Benjamin.

Benjamin's notion of ornament is complex, but its essence resides in the two phrases used by Buck-Morss — 'historical truth' and 'utopian dreams'. What Benjamin was trying to do was understand the rampant historical eclecticism that was nineteenth-century ornament, and in particular comprehend the last flowering of European ornament before its banishment at the hands of the modern. Why was it, he asks, that the new first chose to appear in an area like ornament which, at first sight, appeared so *passé*? His answer lies in his classic description of the temporalities at work in the historical process at certain moments of transition:

> To the form of the new means of production, which to begin with is still dominated by the old [Marx], there correspond images in the collective consciousness in which the new and the old are intermingled. (21)

Historical truth, argues Benjamin, never appears in a 'neat' form where one can find a straightforward congruence between form and content.

Instead, that which is new first emerges within the collective in the clothes of the mythic, but it is a mythic that faces in two directions. One aspect is turned towards the past where it stretches back into the collective's archaic fund of images — its mythos. The other aspect faces towards the future as these archaic elements are thrown forward in time in an attempt to imagine a number of utopian potentialities carried within the new. For Benjamin, nineteenth-century ornamentation was just one of a number of sites where the old and the new could be found in conjunction. So within the register of the ornamental it is possible to discern — in the convolutions and configurations of their materiality — a kind of collective reverie, or more precisely, a sort of collective aspiration straining to give form to that which had not yet come into existence. In this search for an appropriate form for the new, this as yet unformed, immaterial and migratory collective impulse alights upon archaic, even primal, images and it is these that are then projected forward into the future. It is here that we can see what Benjamin means by his observation that 'the new and the old are intermingled'. It becomes a way to imagine the possibility of transforming daily life, a possibility brought about by the arrival of the new forms of technology. Thus the modernist new, before it encased itself in the ideology and style of functionalism, poured itself into that which was about to disappear. At its centre lay an imaginary formulation of Nature as ur-image, iconographic pool, in possession of a phantasmagorical plasticity. It was a constellation within which this collective aspiration could be formulated. The fragments of this imaginary nature could be found scattered across the utopian wishes of the collective. These mythic elements of Nature were re-worked into images that spoke of material abundance, the abolition of class, and a condition where Nature was finally reconciled with order of the human. One area regarded by Benjamin as exhibiting a particularly poignant conjunction of the old and the new was fashion.

The gradual percolation of the rhythms of fashion and the fashionable amongst the middle classes of nineteenth-century Europe was interpreted by Benjamin as the displacement of Nature by the fetishised forms of the commodity cycle. The seasonal rhythms associated with old, organic Nature had begun to disappear, but were called back in the artificial rhythms of fashion's annual cycle. However, Benjamin goes much further than simply issuing generalisations about the new relationships between fashion and nature. It is in the way that he pursues these linkages down into the very forms and details of nineteenth-century women's costume, which makes what he has to say bear directly upon the appearance of the hats. From a general viewpoint, Benjamin construes this last flowering of European ornament as a sort of artificial Nature; old, organic Nature is in retreat, its rhythms no longer congruent with the metabolism of urban capitalism. But in this retreat, Nature and its representational order were rendered available for use by the operations of fantasy and collective reverie. Why was this? It is as if the collective imagination is able to sense the imminent obsolescence of Nature and its representational order. In its very decay there is a loosening of its adherence to the objects of everyday life. This loss of adhesion imparts to the whole ornamental register a mobile quality that was previously lacking. (It is its very obsolescence that allows it 'to float.') In this fluid condition it can be called back and re-played, but now as artificial Nature. The reappearance of Nature within the modality of artifice functions along a number of axes and within several lines of displacement. There is the 'Far away' (the domain of the exotic) and the 'Long ago' (the domain of the mythic). This register of artificial nature becomes the place where nature and humanity are able to be reconciled. It is an area where clothes, their ornamentations, even the wearers themselves, mimic and replay the forms and rhythms of old organic Nature. Thus we arrive at a point where Benjamin's theory of ornament joins our earlier speculations about the decorative and the ornamental. There is, in this re-playing of nature-as-artifice, a space, an interval, in which a number of transformations are enacted. It is the place where artificial Nature is made.

But what does this "artifice" consist of? What kinds of transformations are involved in the production of this extraordinary and bizarre flowering? It might appear that, at first sight, what unfolds upon these hats is nothing more unusual than yet another re-playing of the European tradition of the pastoral. But if it commences as a species of pastoral it quickly strays a long way from the traditional forms characteristic of this genre. At one level we can detect in the movements of artifice on these hats a move from using 'real' natural objects to an ornamental order made up of a schematised Nature. Within this drift a number of stages seem to be present. Initially, there is a fragmentation of an 'original' followed by the switching of various decorative elements between a limited number of categorical opposites. (Making inorganic motifs out of organic material) The final stage consists of the emergence of an artificial order in which the previous distinctions are left behind and where, in the words of Benjamin, 'the human and natural order are reconciled'. Even when the hats used real elements taken directly from nature there was a sense that what was being seen was a natural order that had already undergone some kind of 'adjustment'. They had already been inserted into a system of manipulable and interchangeable units through the practice of trimming. Real, natural elements were used, but they were no longer able to invoke a highly specific set of meanings, only a vague and abstracted idea of nature. The wider and more abstract the field of evocation became, the more a space was opened for 'nature-as-trimmings' to be used within the configurations of these dream pile-ups. History, as a coherent narrative, has decayed into images and these images fragmented even further into units, part objects and free-floating signifiers that were able to be arranged and rearranged without regard for the 'original' from which they were taken. In fact it was precisely this formalisation of the natural order that opened it up to the possibility of a radical re-writing. Once this level of systemisation has been reached, it was possible for trimmings to be arranged in such a way that, what in Nature was distinct and separate, became on the hats, commingled and fused.

The decorative elements on the hats are part of an elaborate series of 'switchings' in which the qualities given to an object by the natural order are altered by moving it across a number of 'unnatural' categories. They become artificial, unnatural. An example of this can be seen in the way in which flowers are transformed by the ever-increasing pressure towards schematisation.

Artificial flowers were used initially to produce an accurate likeness to an original, real flower. However, these 'real' artificial flowers gradually changed into blooms that had no original in nature. The flowers even attempted to improve on nature by opening up a field of parodic flora. If we turn to the fate of fauna on the hats we find that inorganic materials were worked into the forms of insects or miniature birds. In the reverse of this inorganic–organic transaction, organic matter and the parts of once-living creatures could be reworked into geometric patterns and shapes. As we have already seen, barn owls could be 'improved' by dyeing them pink. Real flowers and artificial ones were arranged into patterns that violated (or 'improved' upon) their appearance in Nature. Insects and butterflies' wings were arranged into the cool perfection of the crystalline whilst 'natural' materials such as straw and felt were dyed in a range of startlingly unnatural hues.

The shapes of the natural order could be mimicked by the inorganic just as natural materials could be formed into shapes that were usually associated with the inanimate; feathers were 'adjusted' to form regular patterns; straw was bent into the shape of a bow, or coronet. The exact sequences taken by some of these exchanges became increasingly complex and difficult to follow as the game of artifice intensified. One of the most tortuous of routes is that taken by stuffed creatures. Fiona Clark relates how, in the 1870s, artificial animals were used in hats, but by the 1880s (and this was related to the rise of taxidermy) 'real' but stuffed creatures began to displace the artificial ones. These stuffed animals were often situated within 'realistic' settings that could consist of real found objects or artificial 'natural' objects. When we reach this level of complexity the organic and the animate are being transformed into the inanimate by being stuffed, then re-introduced as a simulacrum of the animate whilst all around them nothing is any longer what it seems. It is at this point that the careful tracing of these apparently endless switchings can only be halted by asking the question, 'What is it that this dance of artifice, where everything appears as its opposite, aspires too?' 'What kind of world is trying to come into being?'

After a certain threshold of transactional complexity has been crossed we are forced to accede to their irresolvable ambiguity. We can no longer account for the hat decorations by simply itemising each motif. The 'disposition' of the totality of the decorations needs to be recognised. Inevitably, we are led to the conclusion that what is happening here is much more than a simple shuttling of trimmings across a number of binaries. What we appear to be dealing with is a third order of nature in which its artificiality consists in the cancelling out of such oppositions, and instead installs their reconciliation. If, as I believe, the artificial does contain an element of fantasy, then it is here that it might be found. It is also here that we might detect the presence of that 'projective' strand that Benjamin regards as constituting the second part of the collective fantasy, the place where 'the old and the new are intermingled'. What is being projected is a third order of Nature that, in its 'elaborate confections', in its miniature world of switchings and transformations, allowed a 'new nature' to emerge in which the organic and the inorganic, the animate and the inanimate, and the human and Nature no longer stand against one another. In the very mutuality of this con-fusion emerges something in which the original oppositions have disappeared. There is a melting of opposites and a mingling of the unlike. Recall Focillon's observations on the order of ornament:

> This strange realm of ornament [the chosen home of metamorphosis] has given birth to an entire flora and fauna of hybrids. (22)

Could we not extend Focillon's notion of hybridisation to include not just a conjoining, within a single entity, of two or more parts taken from different elements of the natural world, but also a conjoining of elements deriving from different categories altogether, in such a way that the animate mingles with the inanimate and the organic and the inorganic change places. For a short while, in a certain place, Nature and humanity were at peace atop of women's heads.

Notes and References

(1) 'By the closing years of the 1870s a new variety of forms and complexity in trimmings was noticeable in hats, reflecting a trend that lasted throughout the 1880s'. Fiona Clark, *Hats* (London: Anchor Press, 1982) pp. 34-35
(2) Clark, *Hats*, p. 37.
(3) *Ibid*
(4) Alison Gernsheim, *Fashion and Reality* (London: Faber & Faber 1963) p. 74. As early as the 1860s the fondness for using the plumage of tropical birds and egrets had been a matter of public concern. *Punch* (of course) lampooned this feather addiction unmercifully (see *Punch*, May 14 1892) In 1885, The Plumage League, whose motto was 'no feathers for decoration', was established to combat the traffic in plumes. In 1889, the Royal Society for the Protection of Birds came into being specifically to protect those species threatened by the trade in feathers

and carcasses. For a history of the anti-plumage movement see Alan Haynes, 'Murderous Millinery', *History Today*, pp. 32-33.

(5) Asa Briggs, 'Hats, Caps and Bonnets', in *Victorian Things*, (Chicago: University of Chicago Press, 1989) p. 264.

(6) P.J. Corfield, 'Dress for Deference and Dissent: Hats and the Decline of Hat Honour', in *Costume*, p. 23 (1989)

(7) Haynes, "Murderous Millinery" *History Today*, pp. 28

(8) Clark, *Hats*, p. 37.

(9) James Laver, *Taste and Fashion: From the French Revolution to the Present Day* (London: G.G. Harrap & Co. Ltd, 1945) p. 122. This point is re-iterated by Elizabeth Ewing. Apropos Edwardian hats, she comments that they were often 'a yard wide, laden with plumes and feathers or with basket-loads of artificial flowers'. See her *History of Twentieth Century Fashion* (London: Batsford, 3rd edn 1986) p. 6.

(10) Clark, *Hats*, p. 44 and Turner Wilcox, *The Mode in Hats and Headdresses* (New York: Charles Scribners and Sons, 1945) p. 144.

(11) Jacques Derrida, 'The Parergon', in *The Truth in Painting* (Chicago: Chicago University Press, 1987).

(12) Derrida, 'The Paregon', p. 53. The quotation is from Kant's *Critique of Aesthetic Judgement* transl. James Creed Meredith (Oxford: Clarendon Press, 1911) pp. 65, 67-6

(13) Ernst Gombrich, *Sense of Order: a Study in the Psychology of Decorative Art* (Oxford: Phaidon, 1984) p. 218.

(14) Quoted in Gombrich, *Sense of Order: a Study in the Psychology of Decorative Art* p. 49. Gombrich references this as being included in Semper's Kleine Schriften (Berlin, 1884) p. 97.

(15) Henri Focillon, *The Life of Forms in Art* (New York: Zone Books, 1992)

(16) See Roland Barthes, *The Fashion System* (New York: Hill & Wang, 1983) pp. 295-96.

(17) Focillon, *The Life and Forms of Art*, p. 67.

(18) Focillon, *The Life and Forms of Art*, p. 66.

(19) Susan Buck-Morss, 'Redeeming Mass Culture for the Revolution', *New German Critique*, no. 29 (Spring/Summer 1983) p. 236.

(20) Susan Buck-Morss, 'Redeeming Mass Culture for the Revolution, *New German Critique* no. 29, p. 238.

(21) Walter Benjamin, *Charles Baudelaire: A Lyric Poet in the Era of High Capitalism*, p. 159.
(22) Henri Focillon, *The Life and Forms of Art*, p. 67.

Chapter Three

Blemish Free: Facial Order and the Use of Cosmetics

The serious artist, according to academic tenets, creates beauty by liberating the perfect form that nature sought to express in resistant matter.

Ernst Kris

Given that the overwhelming use of cosmetics and makeup in the twentieth century has been by women both as indicators of their femininity and as a way to increase their attractiveness, it is hardly surprising that contemporary explanations have tended to appear within the horizon of this recent history. (1) Whilst acknowledging the inevitability of the shadow cast by the near past, in this essay I want to draw attention to the existence of a much older, and much broader, cosmetic dimension at work in the West. It is a dimension whose influence, particularly in its formal propensities, can be detected inside of the more recent use of these materials and practices as aids to feminine beauty. In fact, I want to suggest that it is impossible fully to comprehend contemporary cosmetic and makeup use without taking into account these older practices and the aesthetic upon which they rest.

One way in which this older regime can be brought to light is to remind ourselves of the various ways in which facial adjustments have been used in the past as well as some of the more peripheral contexts in which they are employed today. Despite the enormous shifts that have taken place during the twentieth century in the principles governing the appearance of both men and women, and despite the considerable degree of convergence in the principles governing their public and private clothing, there is as yet no sign that men are about to adopt the cosmetic practices of women. (2) But this sexual division of cosmetic labour has not always been so clear-cut. Whilst it would be disingenuous to claim that, historically, men and women have used cosmetics with equal frequency, there is no doubt that their use by men has not been as rare as might be supposed. The most celebrated male use of makeup was at the French court in the seventeenth and eighteenth centuries. Engagements at court required men to appear with their faces both powdered and rouged. But male use of cosmetics was not simply confined to moments of aristocratic ceremonial. A certain discrete deployment of rouge and powder were perfectly legitimate even for professional middle class men. (3) There have been occasions when male and female cosmetic practices converged and there have been periods when the use of cosmetics, even by women, has been frowned upon to the point where its use has almost vanished amongst the respectable classes. (4) Other cosmetic and makeup practices have been confined to men. For instance, until well into the nineteenth century it was customary for British military officers to go into battle wearing rouge and face powder. This was to hide any signs of fear on the part of the officers from the common foot soldiers. There are reports (probably apocryphal) that during the Crimean War, the Light Brigade charged into the Russian artillery fire heavily made-up. Nor is it only the living that finds themselves being cosmetically prepared. Undertakers quite regularly apply Mortuary Cosmetics to the faces and hands of the deceased in order to simulate the colour imparted to living bodies by the circulation of blood. (5) And what is one to make of the story told of Madame de Pompadour who, in 1764, lay dying. A priest entered the sick room to administer the last rites. With these completed she reached for her makeup, applied some rouge to her face, turned over and died. One wonders for whose benefit were those final touches being made? War and peace, life and death, male and female, young and old; when one surveys the patterns of cosmetic use there appears to be hardly any social group, or dimension of life that at one time or another, has not, or does not, intersect with the materials and techniques that I have called 'facial adjustments'. When viewed from this broader perspective, such adjustments have been concerned with many more things than simply improving female countenances.

Until quite recently the most common model adopted by scholars towards this topic was that of the historical survey. Here the reader would be presented with an account of the changing techniques, materials and attitudes that constituted the cosmetic practices at any particular historical moment. Each historical instance would then be woven into a story in which the grand procession of past facial styles could be seen to unfold 'across the ages'. In surveys of this kind, intellectual coherency was achieved by grounding the story on some variant of a universalising anthropology. So Corson's account of the history of makeup begins thus:

'Throughout recorded history man has painted his face' (6)

Every word in that sentence cries out for a more thoughtful elaboration and none more so than 'painted'. The theoretical mesh needs to be adjusted so that something smaller than the universal, yet larger than the singular cosmetic event, is capable of being formulated. Somewhere between these two positions it should be possible to commence a description of the particularities of distinctive cosmetic traditions without immediately dissolving it into a universal propensity to 'paint the face' or 'decorate the body'. Every stage in the operation of facial adjustment — from the preparation of the materials, the position they are ascribed in the cultural scheme of things (sacred or profane), the techniques of application, indeed the very notion of what constitutes a face, not to mention the aesthetic and formal aims being striven for — all these elements have to be grasped and located within the total constellation of materials and practices. No amount of substitution of 'painted', or synonyms such as 'decorated' or 'ornamented' can overcome the problem set in motion by assuming that certain practises can be constituted as comparable entities. 'To paint' in one tradition is not the same as 'to paint' in another.

The problem can be seen very clearly in the excellent study of self-decoration in the Mount Hagen region of New Guinea undertaken by Marilyn Strathern. (7) This is one of the few studies in which the differences between Western and non-Western practices are both discussed and recognised and where the temptation to universalise them both is resisted. Strathern makes clear that all gestures (cosmetic or otherwise) resonate with, and are constitutive of, quasi-philosophical notions about the world, the self and the formal organization of appearances. Near the start of this essay she observes that, 'Cosmetics in our own culture beautify the body'. (8) (Something quite foreign to the Mount Hageners.) But, once we start to ask such questions as, 'In what does this consist?' or 'What does beautify mean here?' then the notion that a term like 'cosmetics' (or painted, or decorated) is available for general use is brought up with a start. Such words are already too deeply implicated in the ways of the West. It is for these reasons that I have chosen to remain within the Western practices of facial adjustment, and explore what it is that makes this a distinctive tradition.

In her essay, ' "I must put my face on": Making Up the Body and Marking out the Feminine', Jennifer Craik suggests a complex mix of imperatives at work even within contemporary female cosmetic and makeup practices. (9) In the space of a single page the following rationales are presented:

'Make-up not only confirms sexual attractiveness...'

'The process is not simply one of enhancement but entails the construction of an ideal...'

'The range of faces is designed to cover the kinds of occasions and intended impressions that the wearer literally has to 'face' ... ' (10)

In each instance quite different aspects of cosmetics and makeup are being advanced. Sexual attractiveness, confirmation of sexual identity, the pursuit of a facial ideal and the demands of social etiquette are all identified as ends being sought by cosmetics and make up. What I want to explore in the remainder of this essay are those latter two dimensions: facial ideality and social etiquette. It is here, I think, that the distinctiveness of the western tradition can be found. More precisely, it lies within that quite particular set of relationships that exist between the manipulation of the materiality of the world, conceptions of beauty, ideality and social formality.

Cosmetics

English has two equally ranked synonyms to denote these 'facial adjustments': 'cosmetics' and 'makeup'. Each word has a different etymology and each has arrived in the present by a different route. Of the two, it is *cosmetics*, which is the older by far. The *New Shorter Oxford English Dictionary* indicates that its major contemporary meanings, namely 'The art of adorning or beautifying body' and 'a preparation for use in beautifying the face, skin or hair' enter the language in the seventeenth century. (11) However, the pathway taken by the word prior to its appearance reveals a dimension to cosmetic practice that has become obscured in recent times but which survives as a practice common to women. The word derives from the French 'cosmetique' which in turn has its origin in classical Greek. So the sequence goes — cosmetic < *cosmetique* < *kosemtikos* < *kosmein* (to arrange, order, adorn) < *kosmos*. Angus Fletcher has explored the ways in which the semantic overlays explicit in ancient Greek were revivified at the onset of the Renaissance. (12) *Kosmos* came to mean the universe or some similar kind of totality. *Kosmein* referred to a symbol denoting a particular rank within an hierarchy. This eventually came to refer to the badge, or insignia of office, proper to the individual occupying that position. In other words it was concerned with the place that the wearer occupied within the overall scheme of things. Fletcher has suggested that one of the key meanings of the word was the way it indicated how the macrocosm — that is both the place and the manner of the kosmein — intersected with the local and specific, the microcosm. The idea of the 'cosmetic' circled around the way in which the two orders achieved a 'fit'. Fletcher captures exactly the way in which this articulation implied a certain kind of outer appropriateness:

> ...used adverbially and adjectivally the word *kosmos* and its derivatives implied propriety and decorum (*kosmotes*) in dress and manner, since to be adorned according to one's true rank in society would be to conform to propriety. (13)

Thus, cosmetics in this sense are not simply to do with the face. Rather, it was, and is, a term that could encompass the appearance of the whole person — their clothing, their comportment and deportment and the sounds that come out of their mouths. If one adheres to the order implied in the *kosmotes* then one ensures that one is appearing in a composed and appropriate manner. In doing this one also ensures that the proper order of things is confirmed. It was literally and metaphorically a 'fitting in' of the person. The individual achieved this benign condition by exhibiting on their person the principles of the divine order governing the cosmos. But, if we return to the emergence of the word into English we find that its purely descriptive use — as in Bacon's definition of it as the 'art of decoration (of the body) which is called cosmetic' — is almost straight away accompanied by a very familiar refrain, fear of duplicity and deceit. One has only to look at the poems by Swift, 'The Progress of Beauty' (1719) and 'A Beautiful Young Nymph Going to Bed' (c.1731), to see how, what to us might be experienced as a minor anxiety, progressed into a terrible nightmare. (14) Again, Fletcher has been able to pinpoint the Achilles heel of *kosmotes*. If the proper order of things is capable of being embodied in (and is in fact dependent upon) a display of externalities such as dress, manners, speech and insignia, then it can be faked. He observes:

> Notice that there is nothing neutral about the process: to adorn, in the rhetorical sense of *kosmein*, means to elevate a lower rank to a higher one. Dress and costume can become instruments of social climbing, by this process, and in the social sphere if one spots a social climber, an Osric, or a Pamela, one can be sure the ascent is aided by a use of *kosmoi*, whether of speech, manner, or dress. (15)

It is important that this concern about the ability of cosmetics to deceive society and/or a besotted admirer be distinguished from Romantic criticisms of cosmetics as 'artificial' and 'unnatural'. (Ideas that will be explored shortly.) The early critics of cosmetics would not have dismissed their use out of hand. Rather they would have insisted that they be used 'honestly' and 'properly'; that is as essential elements of civilised behaviour.

When seen within this older sense of order and arrangement, cosmeticization does not just mean a superficial attendance to 'surface appearances', or the deployment of a set of techniques, which attend to the outside whilst leaving the inner condition unchanged. Rather, it is a profound concern with surface appearances undertaken so as to ensure local compliance with the wider, universal order. Turning this around, one might say that the process of cosmetics achieved proper order by suppressing, or at least controlling, disorder. As we shall see in a moment this elimination of 'disorder' on the person, but more particularly on their face, remains at the heart of western practices.

Romanticism and Makeup

The word 'makeup' arrives in the English language much later than cosmetics. It appears in the middle of the nineteenth century and initially is a technical term referring to the materials and techniques used by actors to prepare for a theatrical performance. The *New Shorter Oxford* defines it so:

> 'An appearance of a face, dress, etc, adopted for a theatrical performance or other public appearance'. (16)

The widespread elimination of cosmetic use by men, and the steep decline in its use by middle class women during the Victorian period meant that when it did re-emerge as a mass female phenomena in the nineteen twenties and thirties of the last century its significance was permeated by the ethos of stage and film. Styles of faces were mediated by the publicity surrounding individual female film stars. However, the emergence of this new, exclusively female use of makeup was not a simple displacement of the *universe of cosmetics* by the *order of makeup*. Between the eighteenth century and the twentieth lies Romanticism and in particular its notions of expressive individuality and the pursuit of personal authenticity.

The declining use of cosmetics by both sexes during the latter half of the nineteenth century provides one of the clearest indications of the part played by Romantic ideas both in undermining aristocratic standards of public behaviour, as well as ushering in an order of daily life in which 'unadorned' faces were thought appropriate. It was the 'natural' face, or at least the face devoid of the signs of artifice, that was the preferred mode. One consequence of this was that male and female facial appearances became startlingly different. Male facial hair was allowed to grow unchecked whilst cranial hair was only barely kept under control. For women being 'natural' meant dispensing with cosmetics apart, that is, for a discreet application of rice powder and rouge. It is into this Romantic constellation that the modern word 'makeup' intrudes, not the world of cosmetic order. Despite the modern sense of makeup creating a face that increases the sexual attractiveness of its wearer other kinds of facial adjustment are at work. The legacy of Romanticism can be found in the 'un-made face', or at least the face that looks as if it is 'un-made'. It is this that seems to best embody the person's inner truth — 'Makeup designed to bring out the real you'. Something like this has been the holy grail of the modern cosmetics industry. And, as we shall see, a muted version of the cosmetic facial order reappears with the resurgence of the use of makeup in the twentieth century. Make-up in its modern sense is partially cosmetic.

Beauty and its Techniques

The embodiment of order (formality), the expression of inner being and an increase in sexual attractiveness are the three axes along which the western practice of facial adjustment has been elaborated. For the remainder of this essay I want to argue for the persistent presence of the first of these dimensions — the embodiment of an order or, the cosmetic type of facial adjustment. However much the meaning ascribed to the 'adjustment' of the face has altered over the centuries it always seems to have been the carrier of a set of physical operations and formal principles through which an ideal is made to appear on the face. I can illustrate this more clearly by way of illustration I.

In this advertising image it is possible to see the techniques used in transforming the face of the model from a 'before' into 'an after'. To state the obvious ... what is happening is a re-formation of the given face of the model through the installation of a set of 'organisational principles'. The

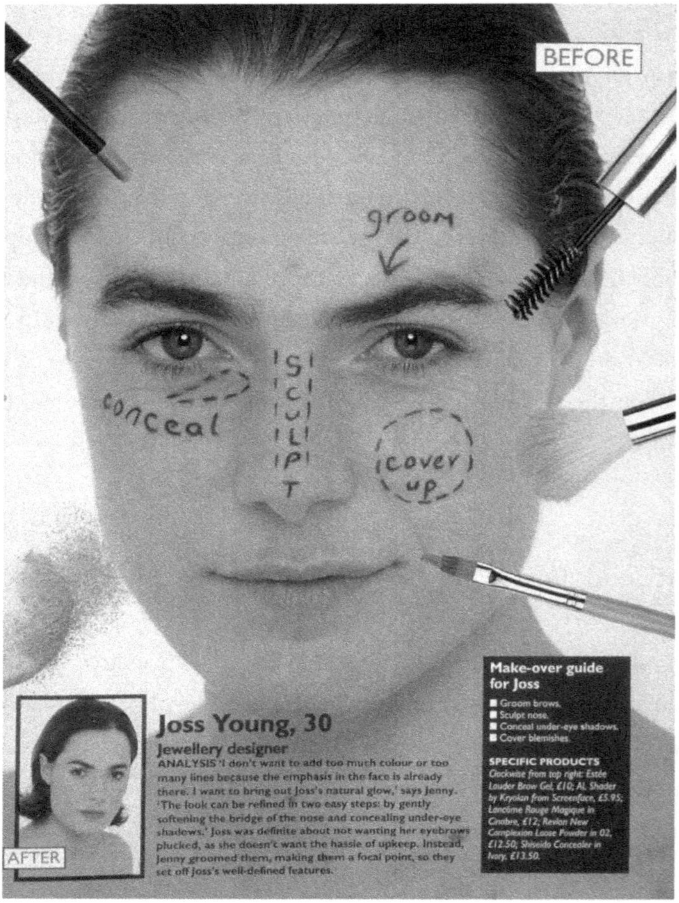

Illustration: 1

Magazine advert. 1998. Sydney.

operation guiding the application of makeup takes the form of an *addition-to* or a *removal-from* the existing facial features. If done correctly, that is if the applier follows the indications on the image, an ideal 'face' should appear from out of the arithmetic sum of additions and removals. (Or more modestly, the original face should approach some way toward that of the ideal.) Among the instructions given by the advert are 'cover up', 'groom' and 'conceal'. This 'sculpting' of the face should not be read as simply an imposition of the currently fashionable female face. Below the fashionable changes in facial styles one may detect a remarkable consistency with regard to the formal (aesthetic) aims being sought, aims that are clearly present in the illustration. Symmetry, proportion, certain homogeneity of colouring and a sharper delineation of line and shape are all persistent formal imperatives. More revealingly we might ask what it is that has to be eliminated, or covered, removed, or disguised in order that a particular face is able to move closer to the desired ideal? What are the exact material techniques employed to achieve these aims?

To suggest an answer to these questions I offer the following observation made by Baudelaire on how makeup works. He says:

> Any enumeration would have to include countless details; but, to limit ourselves to what in our day is commonly called make-up, who can fail to see that the use of rice powder, so fatuously anathematised by innocent philosophers, has as its purpose and result to hide all the blemishes that nature has so outrageously scattered over the complexion, and to create an abstract unity of texture and colour in the skin, which unity, like the one produced by tights, immediately approximates the human being to a statue, in other words to a divine or superior being. (17)

This wonderful observation does suggest a way in which we can draw together the abstractions present in the original idea of the cosmetic and the apparent trivial details of applying makeup to the face. The secret revealed by Baudelaire's indiscretion is that this constitution of cosmetic order is a dual process. It achieves propriety and decorum at the same time as it banishes disorder. (Or as the poet puts it by the 'elimination of blemishes'.) Significantly, in both the general meaning of cosmetics and in Baudelaire's observations of their micro-detail there is a sense that once their correct application has been achieved, the face (and the person) undergoes a significant elevation, existentially, morally and aesthetically. This installation of propriety and decorum over the whole person was congenial because it both embodied and exhibited the wider order of the universe. (The cosmos) With Baudelaire's 'elimination of blemishes' the individual is transformed, becoming approximate to the corporeal perfection of 'a divine or superior being'. In both cases a quasi-divine order arises out of the simple manipulation of physical materials.

To grasp, not only how the elimination of 'blemishes' is achieved through cosmetics, but why it is then able to produce a look of (and a sense of) increased beauty in the 'ordered' individual, we need to integrate these facial adjustments with the totality of operations governing the rest of our appearance e.g. clothes, hair, nails, etc. The intensity with which we carry out these 'grooming' operations varies, of course, with the social situations in which we are required to appear and personal inclination. We are constantly matching our appearance to those variations in formality that are distributed across our daily lives and we take care to 'fit in' with these changing circumstances. A not particularly original generalisation might say that as the degree of formality rises the more we are likely to respond by intensifying our adherence to forms, norms and rules. Put another way, it could be said that a rising level of formality increasingly requires the elimination of the incidental, the particular or the exceptional, or the blemish mentioned by Baudelaire. Everything, that is, that marks us out as singular and so denies us access to the universal. Is it not the case that both the care and the intensity in the application of cosmetics to the female face increases the greater the degree of formality of the social situation in which the person has to appear? (A distant echo of Cecil Beaton's Aunt Jessie perhaps.) Likewise, for the male to appear at a formal occasion unshaven and with hair unkempt, whilst *de rigueur* for young male stars in the entertainment industry, will not do for us little people. Aesthetics and sociology are hard to separate here. Wherever one turns, one encounters a complex interweaving of ideality, beauty, social formality and physical order.

Social, that is collective, formality is accompanied (as the word suggests) by a general movement of the social body from a condition of relative 'unformedness' to one in which a more intense display of form is evident. How this shift is evinced externally takes us to the heart of the cosmetic order. It is not sufficient that formality simply remain a subjective condition. An external formal manifestation is essential in order that a comparative may appear through which both spectators and participants are able to gauge the extent to which the state of 'formedness' has been achieved. In the West (and I suspect in many other cultures) this move from the everyday into the 'ceremonial' has, as its external analogue, an increasing urge to organise the material dimension of the situation into an order in which geometrical regularity, overall symmetry, homogeneity of substance and uniformity of action predominate. It aims at lowering the general level of animation and eliminating (or severely restricting) the occurrence of the incidental and the spontaneous. Movements become highly choreographed. Facial expression is restricted to a very narrow lexicon. Appropriateness of garments may be signalled by a higher standard of cleanliness (absence of stains, spots — those general marks of living which plague the formal) and by their visual precision.

As we noted earlier, Baudelaire suggested that one of the immediate material and spiritual accomplishments of makeup/cosmetics is the elimination of the 'blemish' so as to create an 'abstract unity of texture and colour in the skin'. We have already seen that the idea of a 'blemish' is a broad one and can refer to anything which acts as a hindrance to this 'abstract unity'. The application of cosmetics produces an even, uniform look to the skin, which implies a more perfect condition than that of a face, crowded with incident and surface variations. This superficial uniformity, what might be called the creation of a 'ceremonial face', is emblematic of a higher order than that exhibited by a face that remains enmeshed in the particularities of the everyday. As Baudelaire insisted, the cosmeticized face more nearly embodies the ideal than does the unmade-up one. At first sight this might seem obvious. However, of use in the present context is Baudelaire's willingness to place the divine and the ideal alongside of a set of simple material operations such as the application of rice powder to the face of a woman. The one is an analogue of the other (and I am being deliberately ambivalent about specifying an order of primacy here). Cosmetics consist of a remarkably limited number of strategies to move the face towards this condition of ideality. There is the already discussed imparting of uniformity to the texture of the skin. But as well as this we might cite the regular delineation of edges (eye-brows, eye-lids, and lips). Then there is the imposition of certain homogeneity of colouring and the attempt to create symmetry between the left and right hand sides of the face. If for the moment we simply consider the nature of these physical materials and mechanical operations, then the ideal, which is being striven for, is one in which a certain kind of irregularity must be absent. It is a condition where, as far as appearance is concerned, a certain level of individuality is erased. Or to put it more accurately, we might say that the face is allowed to exhibit certain levels of irregularity, individuality and particularity according to the relative degrees of formality, which any situation demands.

Georges Bataille has argued that under idealistic aesthetic regimes of this kind everything that is particular to an object, or person, comes to be seen as a deviation, or an anomaly. (18) As always with Bataille, what he has in mind here are the ways in which intellectual abstractions and the materiality of the forms of the world, and in particular the forms assumed by us humans, fall into one another. One place where we are able to exert a degree of control over what we might call the 'incidence of blemishing' is in the artefacts we make, the immediate environment in which we live and most poignantly of all, the way we look, move and speak. Clothing in the West has as one of its general functions the alchemical transformation of our particular bodies into something closer to an ideal. (And here I mean texture, pattern, and substantiality, not just profile.) In this sense clothes and all the attendant techniques by which we prepare our appearance are weapons we use to prevent ourselves being perpetually mired in the incidental. Applying cosmetics to the face may be seen as a localised version of the broader aspiration toward the universal. Cosmetics reduce the level of facial individuality in favour of a formal intensity. In doing this the face starts to exhibit a greater degree of similarity to other faces than that permitted by the non-cosmeticized one. In this sense cosmetics replicate on the face what the demands of formality are engendering over the whole person, a hope that, however momentarily, we might touch the divine.

Conclusion

I have attempted to show that cosmetics and makeup can be profitably viewed within that set of techniques that are drawn upon to form the whole appearance of a person. Secondly, and perhaps more importantly, I have tried to show how an ideal order is embroiled in a set of direct and immediate material operations. The straightening out of a line, the delineation of edges, the suppression of a slight change in skin colour, or the erasure a pimple become the material analogues for installing the socially appropriate and the visually attractive. In this sense we can locate cosmetics and makeup within a vast continent of operations where, in our daily lives, we manipulate the stuff of the world to create a material embodiment of some our deepest desires, longings, and anxieties. Not least of these concerns is a kind of proto-aesthetic sensibility of the kind we have seen at work on the face.

The phrase 'tidying up' is wonderfully rich in just such strands of quotidian aesthetics. Is there anything to be learned from the operations of tidying up, say a room, that might shed light on 'fixing a face'? Room tidying consists of a number of related operations. There is the element of cleaning — that is the removal of dirt — analysed by Mary Douglas. (19) There is the element of restoring order where like is placed with like. Finally, each of these operations has an aesthetic dimension; or rather there is an aesthetic strand at work in all the activities classified as tidying up. A room in order to be tidy has also to look tidy. But in what does looking tidy consist of? I would argue that exactly the same formal characteristics we saw operating in cosmetics are present in tidying. A certain geometrical regularity. A certain sharpness of line. Perhaps the covering of disorder with a colourful blanket. Certainly the removal of 'blemishes' by cleaning. In both instances a similar ambiguity is present. In making up a face, or tidying up a room, are we clearing away something that is obscuring its ideal condition, or are we transforming a fundamentally chaotic entity into formal perfection?

Notes and References

(1) One of the most recent, and comprehensive, accounts of makeup in the twentieth century is Kate de Castelbajac, *The Face of the Century: 100 Years of Makeup and Style*, London, 1995.

(2) This raises the question as to whether facial shaving by men can be regarded as a 'cosmetic' practice. I think it can since the term 'cosmetic' can refer to a set of formal principles in which *removal-from* is as much an integral operation as *application-to*. It is the element of *application-to*, which has largely disappeared from male practice.

(3) Richard Corson, *Fashions in Makeup: From Ancient Rome to Modern Times*, London, 1972, p.231:

> 'In the eighteenth century the American colonists of the upper classes were following British and French practice and still importing their cosmetics from Europe. Every gentlemen had his dressing box equipped with shaving necessities, soap, powder puffs, brushes, oil and scent bottles, curling irons, scissors, rouge, if he used it, and often writing materials'.

(4) 'Except for a dash of flowery cologne and a discreet cloud of powder, no lady was suspected of making herself up'.

Castelbajac, p. l2.

There is some evidence that an older cosmetic regime persisted amongst the upper classes until at least the First World War. Cecil Beaton describes his Aunt Jessie getting ready to pay a visit to court so:

> Aunt Jessie would cover her face, neck, arms and back with a thick paint, which by some was called 'enamel', but which my family referred to as white wash. Her eyelids were painted mauve, her cheeks a bright carnation pink, while her lips were cerise.
>
> Cecil Beaton, *The Face of Fashion*, London, 1954, pp.24-25.

(5) My thanks to Mr John Harris Jnr. for the information regarding the use of cosmetics and the dead.

(6) Corson, p. 1.

(7) Marilyn Strathern, 'The Self in Self-Decoration', *Oceania* 49.4 (June 1979): 241-257.

(8) Strathern, p.241.

(9) Jennifer Craik, "' I Must Put My Face On": Making Up the Body and Marking Out the Feminine', in *Cultural Studies:* 1.3 (1989) 1-24.

(10) Craik, "'I Must Put My Face On"...', p. 12.

(11) *The New Shorter Oxford Dictionary*, Oxford, 1993, p.520.

(12) Angus Fletcher, *Allegory: the Theory of a Symbolic Mode,* Ithaca, 1964. See esp. chap.2, 'The Cosmic Image', pp. 70-146.

(13) Fletcher, p. 112.

(14) Swift is disturbed both by the deceit created by the application of cosmetics and the horrors revealed by its removal.

> 'Thus, after four important hours
> Celia's the wonder of her sex;
> Say, which among the heavenly powers
> Could cause such marvellous effects.'
> 'The Progress of Beauty'

> 'Returning at the midnight hour;
> Four Storeys climbing to her bower;
> Then, seated on a three-legged chair,
> Takes off her artificial hair:
> Now, picking out a crystal eye,
> She wipes it clean, and lays it by'.
> 'A Beautiful Young Nymph Going to Bed'

(15) Fletcher, pp. 118-119.

(16) *New Oxford Shorter Dictionary*, p. 1673.

(17) Charles Baudelaire, *Baudelaire: Selected Writings on Art and Artists*, trans. P. Charvet, London, 1972, p.427.

(18) 'The composite image (of the human face) would thus give a kind of reality to the necessary beautiful Platonic idea. At the same time, beauty would be at the mercy of a definition as classical as that of the common measure. But each individual form escapes this common measure and is, to a certain degree, a monster'.

Georges Bataille, 'The Deviations of Nature', in *Visions of Excess: Selected Writings, 1927-1939*, ed. Allan Stoekl, Minneapolis, 1985.

(19) Mary Douglas, *Purity and Danger: An Analysis of Concepts of Pollution and Taboo*, Harmondsworth, I 966.

Chapter Four

Why do Stone Age People Wear Furs?

Introduction

I want to begin with a few introductory remarks about the form taken by this chapter. At its centre is a picture of what we will call the *Stone Age Family*. Each of the sections is a response to, and a meditation upon, different aspects of this Palaeolithic scene, especially the furs they are 'wearing'. The semi-independence of each section inevitably means that some repetition happens — for instance Darwin's adventures in Tierra del Fuego.

Finally, mention must be made of the frequent use of quotation marks. The reader will find that they cluster around those words describing objects placed on the body. Words such as garment, dress, clothes, drape and wear more often than not refer to objects and activities whose meanings derive from them being part of a fully realised, Western, dress regime. They assume a *fait accompli* whilst a great deal of what we will be discussing is to do with those liminal states that existed prior to the advent of mature dress practices. Since a new, pre-clothing vocabulary is out of the question, I have had to make do with the quotation marks that are there to remind the reader not to take the meaning of these strategic words for granted. For instance, to describe someone as being clothed in a context where 'clothes' have not yet appeared causes some difficulties for explanation. The situation examined in this essay is one where the conclusion comes before the evidence.

The Scene

(Illustration 1)
The Family

This illustration appears in *The First People on Earth*, published in 1965 in London by Paul Hamlyn. The author is John Boddington and the artist is Mario Logli. Beneath the picture is the following caption.

> 'From the earliest days, men, women and children have loved to gather round a fire.'

First Furs

We begin with a simple depiction of a Stone Age family taken from *The First People on Earth*, a book intended for 10 to 14 year olds. A male figure attends a fire, while a female sits against a tree caring for a baby, who appears to have fallen asleep. Both adults are 'wearing' animal hides, while the baby is buried deep in the fur of its mother's 'garment'. Aside from the fire, the furs are the most conspicuous feature of this family gathering.

No place or date is given for the scene, but an educated guess would suggest the depicted family were living in northern Europe during the last Ice Age, probably surviving by following the abundant game that existed as the ice sheet retreated. The furs are 'worn' as protection against the biting temperatures of that place and time. This Eurocentric geography — and there can be no doubting the racial origins of the figures — and the amelioration of cold, are the two constants holding up this 'drama of dress', as they are with many others. (Ian Gilligan is an honourable exception to this; although the geographical location shifts to Tasmania, Gilligan's response is still one of creating protection against the cold. (1) To my knowledge, no other sort of clothing response has been considered; for instance, clothing was used as protection against extremely high temperatures. Although the cold response is couched in neo-Darwinian terms, the origin of clothing has never been conceived of in terms of those other classic strategies, natural selection: disguise and camouflage.

Even a preliminary examination of the furs reveals the presence of a number of assumptions (beliefs) as to what kind of objects they are. For instance, the furs appear to have been minimally prepared; only the inside of the skins appear to have received some supplementary treatment, or so we imagine, since we hardly ever catch sight of the 'interior' side of the skin. This is confirmed by the fact that the wearers' bodies show no signs of slaughter, which would be the natural consequence of wearing untreated furs. The skins are always depicted with the fur side out. This convention ensures the animal origins of the furs are both strong and clear, even though wearing the fur inside would be equally efficient in keeping the wearer warm. No matter how much variation there is in the shape and form of the 'worn' skins, the implication remains the same: The journey from skinning the animal to clothing the bodies of the hunters is a short one. From beast to back takes no time at all. How the figures 'wear' the furs, or rather hang them on their bodies, suggests that these primitive people are the product of a way of life bereft of any techniques of refinement. Their ability to further modify the skins is hardly evident. The crudely prepared furs speak of commencements, of beginnings, of prototypes. They are the *first garments*; they have no antecedents. They are the outcome of the most elementary of techniques.

The picture of the world in which our Stone Age family lives is one of brutal immediacy. But this does not quite match the alternative picture that emerges when the fur garments are regarded as *made objects* rather than elements circulating in an historical illustration. If we think about what is required to bring these 'primitive garments' into being, it becomes clear that a far more complex technology is needed than that implied by the 'fast-fur' model. For instance, the woman is wearing a garment joined at the shoulder and, judging by the way it hangs, the pelts have been cut to the same length at knee level. The man is wearing a pelt that may have been sewn together to form a tubular garment, or else it may just be a type of wrap-around. He wears a waistband that appears to be a strip of leather, which may hold up the pelt, and has been more intensively treated than his other furs. If, in reality, 'prehistoric humans' produced and wore such garments they would have required a toolkit of considerable sophistication, and have possessed the skills to use it. To prepare the pelts would have required hunting techniques, tools for skinning the animals, and scrapers and tools for preparing and shaping the hides. Needles and thread would have also been needed to join the pelts. Even if such garments were ever worn, they could only ever have been the product of a complex set of skills rather than the productive immediacy implied by the Stone Age family. It is the form and materiality of the fur that is crucial to this picture of prehistoric humans, not the technology of its making.

The act of killing, skinning and wearing furs elevates humans above animals. In effect, humans are saying: 'We are wearing the skins of the animals in whose world we were recently co-habitants.' They have become able to take the skins of the animals and transform them into a useful means of keeping warm. Despite being only just free of the grip of nature, prehistoric people use furs as bodily protection and this is a sign they are starting to move toward *us*. As yet, the emergence of the human from the animal is very gradual. The early bands of Homo sapiens carried fur on their backs as an emblem of where they had come from; these barely transformed animal skins are signs that the journey towards us has begun.

When, during the 19th century and most of the 20th century, Europeans tried to imagine what the first Homo sapiens were like, they invariably put them in animal furs despite there being no evidence for this. The remainder of this essay asks why this was so.

Archaeology: The Evidence

In all probability, by the time the reader encounters this section of the essay it will already be out of date. Such is the rate at which material relevant to body supplementation is being uncovered. Modern archaeological techniques have ensured the recovery of evidence pertinent to dress, which previously would have gone undetected. Nevertheless, direct evidence of the 'bodily adjustments' of early humans does remain exceedingly scarce. This means speculation of one sort or another is an inevitable consequence of building a picture of how early humans regarded their bodies.

Over the past 20 years or so, archaeologists have been making discoveries associated with the preparation and use of materials that appear to be associated with 'body decoration', or 'body ornament'. They point to marks or objects — ochre and beads — that are placed on the body for a variety of reasons. But what might be happening has never really been subject to speculative elaboration and remains obstinately vague. These materials and their use also have a more general significance, raising the question of what kind of relationship early men and women had towards their bodies. The archaeological finds, and their significance, have become crucial elements in a far-ranging debate about the origins of what archaeologists call 'cultural modernity'. In other words, body alterations are part of a number of activities that mark the appearance of 'modern' humans.

Archaeology, Clothing and Body Decoration

Clothing — that is, garments made of cloth — is generally thought to be a product of the Neolithic revolution and the invention of weaving around 10,000 BC. The body covered with clothing enabled it to assume a variety of 'non-natural' shapes; it also enabled it to acquire a decorated surface through ornamentation being woven into, or placed onto the fabric. However, E. W. Barber has argued that from the end of the Ice Age (40,000–35,000 BC in Europe) until the Neolithic revolution, 'the string revolution', as she calls it, took place. (2) The string she sees as so crucial was used to thread beads into lengths of a metre or more. These could then be used to form proto-textiles, with 'sheets' of beading placed on the body. Barber has even detected a 'string' apron on one of the European Venus figurines dated to about 20,000 BC. (Illustration 2) If we move back in time to about 40,000–35,000 BC, beads (very often made from shells) start to lose the 'ghost' of clothing — a covering sheet — although some elements of 'stringing' technique must have remained. Beads have been found in excavations undertaken in such disparate regions as the Middle East, Kenya and South Africa. They are currently (in 2012) dated back as far as 75,000 BC, with archaeologist Marie Vanhaeren even placing some finds at 1000,000 BC. (3)

One final piece of evidence that must be mentioned is the use of ochre (red and/or black) to decorate the body. One reason for its use was that only a very simple set of tools and techniques was required to prepare it. Burial sites are one of the most common places it has been detected, the soil presumably stained from the ochre smeared on the corpse. Blocks of what might be called ready-to-use ochre have been found in widely distributed settlement sites. These forms of ochre use have in some cases been dated to before 100,000 BC. Regardless of the presence of ochres, the interpretation of its use in body decoration has been challenged. One guess as to its significance is that it was a way of aiding a group or an individual through periods of profound change, where new bodily forms were required; hence the role it might play in the burial 'service'. But like all speculation it remains open to counter-claims.

Despite current debates about the when and where of body decoration, there is a degree of agreement as to its relationship with other kinds of more recent 'human' behaviour. These 'new' areas of human life are referred to as 'cultural modernity', and along with body decoration its markers include language, art, music, dance, the capacity to think symbolically — although there is considerable debate as to what form this took — and the incest taboo. Georges Bataille has described the emergence of these forms of behaviour as evidence that the human species was at last capable of living in ways 'that went beyond the demands of immediate usefulness'.

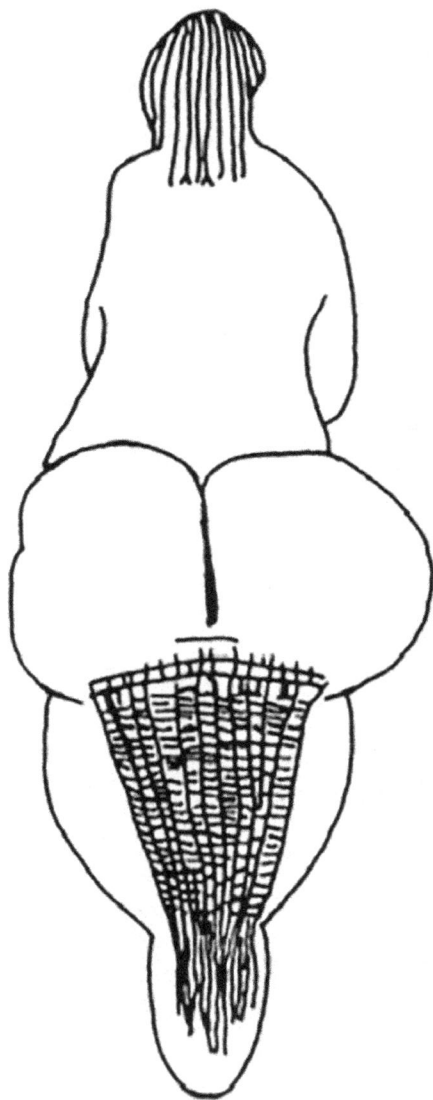

Illustration 2: European 'Venus" figurine. 20,000 BC

But it is Marian Vanhaeren who has put forward the boldest explanations for the earliest beads found so far; she has isolated 14 possible reasons for the presence of these beads, ranging from the vague but intriguing activity of 'beautifying' through to being used as units in forms of exchange. She relates the proliferation of bead use to the rise of a 'modern' social order, with a set of internal differentiations and collective functions. For Vanhaeren, the beads were units that existed to circulate through a group and between groups, in a manner similar to the 'total institution' proposed by Marcel Mauss. (4)

For the most part, the archaeological fraternity seems content to use such words as 'beautify', 'ornament' and 'decoration' in a largely uncritical manner. Little consideration has been given to the rich and complex layers of meaning compacted into words such as these. At a minimum, some consideration ought to be given to what takes place when the body moves from an undecorated state to a decorated one. These semantic excavations deserve an approach just as careful as excavations in the field demand. To put it crudely: why paint, smear or attach stuff to your body in the first place? What was it that tilted, at a certain point, human beings into 'adjusting' their bodies in these ways? Why was it that the daily round we were given by nature was considered insufficient?

When one surveys the evidence supporting the existence of early forms of clothing, let alone body decoration, the only way to approach the matter is via controlled speculation. If we return to the figures in their furs, we are confronted with the problem that there is currently little or no evidence that in reality they were 'clothed' in animal furs. The picture is not only historically inaccurate but, in the parlance of earlier times, fanciful. There is some slight direct evidence for clothes being made — for instance, the perforated needles found at the Sunghir burials in Russia, dated to 22/25,000 BC — but this is a long way from 'proving' animal furs were used as the first human garments. Humans were portrayed wearing furs a long time before there was any evidence to support the historical veracity of the Stone Age scene. The furs arrived before the evidence. So what was it that brought them into being, and what was it that endowed these garments with the power to persist for more than 150 years?

The Horror

In 1832, Charles Darwin, on his voyage around the world on H.M.S. Beagle, recorded his first impressions of the native people of Tierra del Fuego. Forty-two years later the memory of the Fuegians still made his blood run cold.

> The astonishment which I felt on first seeing a party of Fuegians on a wild and broken shore will never be forgotten by me, for the reflection at once rushed into my mind — such were our ancestors. These men were absolutely naked and bedaubed with paint, their long hair was tangled, their mouths frothed with excitement, and their expression was wild, startled and distrustful.
>
> Charles Darwin: *The Descent of Man,* 1874 (5)

Neanderthal

Ever since the remains of Neanderthals were first discovered in Europe in the first half of the 19th century, scientific discussion about the nature of these people has been dominated by the relationship they had with Homo sapiens. The aim of this comparison has been to establish the degrees of similarity and difference between the two populations. Much more was at stake than producing cool scientific knowledge; investigations carried out within this comparative framework had implications not only for

Neanderthals but also for Homo sapiens — for us.

The Neanderthal discoveries were drawn into a sometimes-fierce argument about what it means to be human: Who and what are we? The foundation of these shifting comparisons lies in the contrast between Neanderthal skeletal remains and the skeletons of Homo sapiens. When skeletal difference — therefore, morphological distinctiveness — was being emphasised, Neanderthals were regarded as more simian, so less 'advanced', than their sapient cousins (see ill. 3); this skeletal primitiveness was accompanied by a cruder cultural repertoire than that of Homo sapiens. This position reached its pinnacle in the long-held belief that the superiority of Homo sapiens enabled them to wipe out Neanderthals through violent confrontation, or by displacing them from food-rich territories to unproductive margins where they died out.

The perceived difference between the two populations has ebbed and flowed ever since Neanderthal remains were first uncovered. Most disputes about the significance of the growing archive of Neanderthal remains have flared up when new evidence appears to draw Neanderthals closer to Homo sapiens. This evidence includes the possibility of funerary practices, the use of red ochre as body decoration and, most controversial of all, and the assertion that Neanderthals had language. All of these practices, if they did exist, threaten to place Neanderthals in the category of cultural modernity, a status that Homo sapiens jealously guard for themselves.

When it comes to imagining what Neanderthals might have looked like — that is, when pictorial depictions are attempted — we once again find that furs and pelts have insinuated themselves into the imagery (see ill. 4). Depicting Neanderthals presents the artist with some difficulties. If the difference between Neanderthals and Homo sapiens is thought of as considerable, to depict them as having skin 'garments' brings them too close to 'us'; to show them running about naked seems to be the answer. Neanderthal people are, however, rarely depicted and this may be because there is an imperative to maintain the comparison, so as to appreciate 'what a piece of work is man'. The Neanderthal has 'garments' but they are of a much cruder construction than those imagined for Homo sapiens. Not only are animal materials placed on the body, they are placed around the genitals, in line with our modesty regime. The implication of covering the male genitals, for it is usually males who are depicted, seems to pass without notice. Again there is no evidence for such 'garments', but one could speculate about where they came from. The discovery that Homo sapiens carry a portion of Neanderthal DNA has given rise to some interesting speculations about how this genetic co-mingling came about. Perhaps they are not as 'other' to one another as had been supposed. One of the cultural crossovers between Homo sapiens and Neanderthals might be the 'civilising' of the latter, which showed them to cover up.

(Since initially writing this section an alternative explanation of the shared DNA has been advanced. Neanderthal and Homo sapiens may have a shared ancestor as far back as 500,000 years BC 'Neanderthals and humans have a common ancestor.' Guardian Weekly, 24-08-12)

Invention

'All in all, though humans differ but little from other animal species, no more than the latter differ from other animal species, no more than the latter differ from one another, that difference has mighty consequences for the world we inhabit, since it is a world that, to an ever greater extent, we have made for ourselves, and that confronts us as the artificial product of human activity.'

T. Ingold. (ed.) *What is an Animal?* (6)

If we were to travel from the time and place of the pictured Stone Age family along the line of '30,000 generations' of historical continuity, we would eventually enter a world where furs were no longer worn. How the furs came into being depends upon what one believes they are, and it is this that will flow into the gap between the presence and absence of the furs. Change the definition of what sort of objects the furs are, and their 'events' and coming into being within the historical space will change too.

Illustration 3
Artists Impression: male Neanderthal
Source: TechEYE.net, 12 January 2012

The depiction of the Stone Age family is *historical* in two ways. First, it shows a scene located temporally 'back there', and we are invited to view it as if we were unseen visitors watching the family's daily round; while we look at the figures we remain outside of the events depicted. Second, the picture also has a more direct relation to us, located in our 'here and now'. The scene directly sets up a relationship between 'then and now'. Individuals who are our ancestors, who became us, people the picture. We are what they became. The 'we' in that sentence is guaranteed by the racial characteristics of the figures: they, and we, are early Europeans.

But if we are what they have become, can we then ask what, or rather who, was it that became the Stone Age people. With fur 'garments' being, as we have seen, perhaps one of the most important signs of 'humanity', the way in which they are thought to have come into being colours how one makes sense of the people they are intended to 'clothe'. The prehistoric shadow cast backward by the scene is not just a place where a certain kind of object is 'invented'; it is also the space where we, too, were formed.

Most scientific explanations — see, for example, Ian Gilligan's work on prehistoric clothing and Tasmania — of how and why clothing came into existence rest on the assumption that clothing is first and foremost a technological object, a useful tool, something capable of providing the wearer with protection against the cold. (7) In this model of invention, for that is what it is, a specific environment will throw up a problem that the group or individual must 'respond' to with a solution. In the case of clothing, the most common problem is thought to be a drop in temperature and the successful response is the invention of clothing. At this point, the explanation swings into a variant of the theory of natural selection. A successful invention will confer advantage on those who responded to the problem, who then embed the solution more deeply into their toolkit where it undergoes a process of refinement over time. A response is always couched in terms of its usefulness in relation to the survival of the group or species. But if we turn to such things as decoration, or if we entertain a notion of 'clothing' that far exceeds the utilitarian model, then the *problem, response, invention, advantage* sequence will not do. Only after some brutal surgery on those dimensions of human life that are not primarily technological may they be made to 'fit' the invention/natural selection model.

If clothing and bodily decoration arise from separate roots then it is easy and legitimate to see 'clothing', in the form of furs, as a response to the cold: a tool for bodily protection. But if we see clothing and bodily decoration, in its widest sense, as having a common root then a purely utilitarian explanation seriously distorts matters. Rather than simply a technical view of clothing, where it sits within a network of technical relationships and is ruled by a calculus of efficiency, *dress* may be an essential component of transforming the human body into forms other than those bestowed by nature. Dress is part of a wealth of relationships between parts of the physical environment, between men and women and between generations. Dress and dressing are just one aspect of a broader, collective remaking of our world, where being dressed enables us to enter and take our place in a 'remade' universe. Dress is part of an extensive and complex web of rites, symbols and practices that 'make' us what we are. These cannot be rationalised into a common currency of survival, or technological advantage. Our 'dress' is a complex amalgam of material assemblages, with social tasks, metaphysical aspirations and a poetry all its own.

Dressed or Clothed?

Description lies at the heart of understanding something so mundane and yet so extraordinary as the ways in which we dress and 'appear'. Description relies on language and sometimes, as in the case of how we 'adjust' our bodies, it can fail to accurately map the varied conditions the body may find itself in. Even more bewildering is the fact that there is often no consensus regarding how words relevant to the topic may be used. These considerations come into play when we attempt to describe what members of the pictured Stone Age family have on their bodies. Straight away the questions start to pile up: Are they *wearing* the furs or are the furs simply draped over them? Are they 'wearing' clothes, garments, dress or fashion, or just a useful artefact? Is it different to wear something rather than to drape it? We have already drawn attention to the liminal position occupied by the Stone Age family, and to the way in which much vocabulary we use to describe elements of our dress is inadequate when it comes to describing what members of the Stone Age family have on their bodies. Again we need to ask: Are they clothed or are they dressed? Are they wearing clothes, and, if not, how do we describe what they have on their bodies?

In December 1832, HMS *Beagle* sailed into Good Success Bay, in Tierra del Fuego. On board was a young Charles Darwin, who had been hired as a companion for the ship's captain, Robert Fitzroy. They had two tasks to fulfil: the first, an official one, was to continue mapping the area for the Admiralty; the second, an unofficial task, was to return to their tribe three Yamana (Fuegian) Indians who had been taken to Britain on an earlier expedition. Two observations made by Darwin have become legendary. The first is his description of a Yamana man approaching him 'naked', but for snowflakes settling on his body. The other is his description of the Yamana as the most 'abject', 'degraded' and 'wretched creatures' he had ever encountered — a feeling that lasted for the rest of his life. It is clear that as far as Darwin was concerned the two conditions — 'naked' and 'abject' — were intimately connected. (8)

There is no doubt that Darwin was appalled by the lack of clothing. Yet, when one reads the various accounts he wrote of his encounters with the Indians it is clear that things were not quite as they seemed. While constantly describing the Yamana as 'naked', Darwin simultaneously seemed aware that they were not totally bereft of bodily 'adjustments'. For instance, he remarks: 'The women are naked apart from a flap of skin about their middles'. Sentences like this occur time and time again: 'naked apart from...', 'naked but for...' The problem seems to be that there was, and is, no category between clothed and naked for him to draw on. Countless European explorers had relied on the presence or absence of clothing to guide their judgments about the indigenous populations they encountered. For instance, Columbus records that the Carib natives he encountered were naked *except for* their use of body paint and complex hairstyles. For the Europeans, only clothes counted. Bodily markings were regarded as nothing more than primitive self-decoration, no different to the tattoos that, according to Adolf Loos, were so favoured by the lower orders of European society. So the question that Darwin and his fellow Europeans have left us with is this: If the Yamana are neither naked nor clothed, then what condition are they in?

Detailed study of the Selk'nam (also labelled naked), a tribe living close by the Yamana, has revealed a group of people who made wide use of the materials of their immediate environment. They had a complex, collectively endorsed set of bodily practices, which involved perhaps only one element that could be described as clothing. These were the skins of the guanaco they hunted, and these were more draped than worn. (9)

Confronting such bodily decorations, European adventurers saw nothing more than primitive decoration and ornament, the products of peoples sunk in savagery. It is clear that words such as 'decoration' and 'ornament' do not have the fine semantic mesh required to grasp the totality of bodily activities practised by people such as the Selk'nam. But there is one relevant strand of meaning that can be extracted from decoration and ornament, and that is the sense that they involve an activity that *positively transforms* some object or other. To decorate a body is to positively transform it. This sense of bodily transformation encompasses both the clothed condition of Europeans as well as that of the Selk'nam and the Yamana. There is a word that can be applied to both clothed and non-clothed bodily states, and that word is *dressed*. The Yamana that Darwin met were not clothed, but they were dressed. There were practices for the maintenance of the properly dressed state: Every few days the Yamana would wipe their bodies clean of old guanaco fat and paint, and then apply a fresh layer. Is this not equivalent to our washing and ironing, an appearing new? Being dressed, in this sense, refers to the results produced by a series of activities performed on the body to bring it into a desired state. Nowhere does this necessarily involve wearing that particular class of objects called clothes.

The question we began with was how one would describe the figures in the picture: Are they dressed or clothed? What should we call the furs they have placed around their bodies? We have seen that that 'being clothed' is just one variant of the far wider bodily condition of 'being dressed'. Common to these conditions is a transformation — a readying, a preparation — of the body. The figures in the picture, however, appear not to be engaged in a transformation of this kind. They are clothed in such a way that no transformation of their bodies has taken, or will take, place. The figures do not project forward into a transformed state but remain stuck in a pre-social condition. The bodies and the furs seem stubbornly indifferent to one another, unable to achieve the kind of synthesis and transformation that is accomplished by being dressed. Rather than being dressed or clothed, they are depicted in an impossible state. To be clothed without being dressed is only possible within the licence of the image, which purports to depict the bodily adjustments (furs) before, or without, the social milieu in which they make an appearance. Even if the furs were 'invented' as a protection against the cold, they could never appear shorn of the marks of their symbolic environment.

Dressing

How to Dress a Rabbit
Slit across the back.
Pull apart (skin) from hind legs.
Pull skin/fur away from body.
Remove head and feet.
Separate head from fur.
Slit across belly.
Tease out intestines.
Remove liver and inspect.
Remove kidneys and Diaphragm.
Remove heart and lungs.
Break pelvis (on both sides)
Remove genitalia and tail.
Check for debris and wash.
Rabbit may be hung for a week or more in a dry, cool place to improve its flavour.

From www.ukrabbiter.co.uk

Not all the transformations brought about by dressing are voluntary and benign. There are compulsory forms of dress that are forcibly imposed upon a group and maintained through coercion. Whilst not as common as the banning of a population's native language, there are certainly numerous examples where authentic native costume is forbidden in favour of a politically approved alternative. It is certainly the case that some sorts of dressing can obliterate, not liberate, the spirit.

On a visit to the National Museum in Port Vila in the early nineties I came across an exhibition of photographs taken in the latter part of the nineteenth century. On the left hand wall were pictures of the locals dressed in traditional costume. On the right hand wall were photographs of some locals dressed in European garments. Whilst being aware of the dangers of interpreting these images through the lens of an anti-missionary disposition, there can be little doubt that the 'civilized' individuals looked as if their spirit had left them. The missionaries had initially insisted that the native populations be dressed in a European fashion because they were under the impression that the native forms of dress left them naked. Little, or no, legitimacy was given to indigenous forms of dress; instead the men were often dressed in ill-fitting suits, Shirts, buttoned up to the neck but no ties. The ensemble was finished off with poor imitations of European haircuts. The women, at the instigation of the missionaries, wore drab, floor length dresses and European hairstyles. This preparation through clothing was to produce individuals who were both covered up and so fit for a pious Christian life. Being 'clothed' was a moral condition, not just a physical state. But the contrast between the figures on the left, dressed in ways that seemed to elicit joy from the wearers was in contrast with the abandoned individuals on the right. As they gazed across the gallery space they seem consumed by a terrible sadness as they contemplated their loss of the sacred.

Style

'Nathan Clark, the inventor of the desert boot, was a lifelong enthusiast for shoemaking, technically curious and inventive, with an eye for that simplicity, so hard to achieve around the aesthetic-practical compromise that is the human foot'.

Obituary
Guardian. 4th July. 2011.

Archaeologists acknowledge that even some of the earliest stone tools have a distinctiveness clear enough for them to be grouped together in regional and temporal groups. This distinctiveness may simply be the outcome of their being multiple pathways to mechanical efficiency or, as is more likely, it indicates the presence of that constant companion to human making, namely, style. Whilst it is not unusual for mechanical efficiency to be sacrificed for considerations of style, the majority of human products will always be 'styled' in some way or another. If we turn to the Stone Age Family two questions present themselves. What is style? Are the furs worn by the figures 'stylish'?

Susan Sontag has offered one of the best answers to the question of 'What is Style?' At the very end of her essay 'On Style' she says:

> 'Whenever speech or movement, or objects exhibit a certain deviation from the most useful, insensible mode of expression or being in the world, we may look at them as having style.'

Sontag's definition makes a clear distinction between the 'deviations' that are style and what they are deviating from. The dimension of *non-deviation* comes close to the categories of the utilitarian and the functional that are in use in this investigation. The universe of non-deviation is a world with the creases ironed out and where the shortest distance between A and B is always a straight line. Here form definitely follows function. Style then, is an area that exceeds the determinisms of use and function. (10)

More Characteristics of Style

Style is a collective phenomenon. It is repeated. It spreads. There are no styles of just one. Most styles do not have a recognisable point of origin. They are authorless. Metaphorically speaking, style exercises a certain control over the 'hand' of the maker and guides the 'line' along stylish directions.

Style is related to the fact that what is made by humans always merges into, and within, a social and cultural 'context'. Human things do not float in a vacuum. Nothing made by human beings can escape style.

It refuses to take the shortest route from A to B except where the style wishes to mimic the functional.

Style may be understood in a general sense, that is has a presence in the full range of man-made things, actions, speech, movement and sound and the significance that a specific style has for its audience.

It remakes the world in forms other than those of nature. It imparts to the world a sense of rightness.

The family group is depicted as if they were living in a 'style less' world, a place where there is nothing to spare for, to use Sontag's phrase, those 'certain deviations'. They are 'dressed for utility, not for style. This choice of function over style has a number of important implications for how the lives of prehistoric people are viewed. Style is that point, or moment, where the natural and the man-made part company. Are the furs simply useful remnants taken from the corpses of animals or are they things that have been made and shaped in ways that are obeying imperatives over and above those of use? The depiction of the furs as a *utilitarian* response to the wearer's environment draws upon an evolutionary hierarchy where function and use are assumed to come before, and are more fundamental than, qualities such as style. But as mentioned earlier, the archaeological evidence seems to confirm that style was present 'early on' in the emergence of Homo sapiens. Human beings have found it impossible to respond to their world in a 'style-less' manner. Perhaps the most important evolutionary element is that style signals the presence of an elementary form of freedom. It both allows and guides the creation of 'stuff' beyond the powerful insistence of nature and use. Style is one of the first parts of a human life devoted to ends that lie beyond survival. What comes into being with the emergence of style, is a parallel order where the given makes way for the desired.

The depiction of the figures 'dressed' in a style-less style corresponds to the depiction of the family as being clothed in utility alone. Both are impossible situations for any human artefact because dress, tools, etc always

100

emerge within a social order of some kind and this means encountering symbolic fields of varying degrees of complexity, which in turn means that they will always have more than a utilitarian significance.

Why Do Men and Women Dress Differently?

The Stone Age scene is not just an inaccurate' historical picture waiting to be corrected from our cognitively superior vantage point. It is a picture of the 'past' intended for the present (1965) and aims to show how these, apparently simple, clothing differences came into being. Perhaps nowhere else is the presence of the 'here and now' in the past so evident than in the portrayal of the figures as members of what seems to be a nuclear family. (With the addition of a fitted kitchen the figures could be our contemporaries who have strayed into a fancy dress party.) This is the representation of a way of life whose daily tasks are conducted within a sexual division of labour and where gender differences in appearance could flourish. It is a division/difference that would undoubtedly spread both deeper and wider than simply determining the contents of a work roster. It is more likely to indicate a difference in ways of being.

If we examine the furs worn by the male and female figures it is not hard to enumerate the similarities and differences of what they are 'wearing'. Perhaps the most fundamental feature of the furs is that both male and female are 'wearing' them. The artist has depicted both sexes as having crossed the threshold of 'pre' clothing. Both sexes share in the general movement away from, and out of, the determinisms of the natural order. From here on it is the differences between the two 'ensembles' that stand out. This can be seen in the variation in the colour of the furs, which might imply that the male and the female appear to be wearing the skins of different animals. Is it possible that this is an early example of gender specific materials or, as is more likely, the artist transporting current textile differentiation back to the Stone Age? The most prominent difference between the two sets of fur is in their shapes. The relatively simple construction of the male garment contrasts with the more complex cut and shape of that worn by the woman. Whether this 'female' shape is dictated by the rules of modesty governing female 'garments', or whether it is part of a generic tradition to depict female furs as more complicated than the male is difficult to tell. What constitutes a feminine fur is a fusion of materials, shape, cut, etc, and an exclusive modesty regime played out on the body of a woman. Perhaps nowhere is it so clear that when we look at the Stone Age scene we are looking at early versions of ourselves.

The not inconsiderable difference between the furs of the man and those of the woman begs the question as to how much these 'outfits' are violations of the 'iron law of utility' formulated by Alfred Wallace (1823-1913) and since refined by numerous evolutionary biologists. If the furs 'worn' by the two figures are responses to a drop in temperature why aren't they similar? In other words, to what extent do these furs violate the law of utility and its corollary, the tendency towards an improved efficiency, in favour of the material elaboration of sexual differentiation? Although both are depicted as two different responses to the 'call of the cold', it is to their opposite number, and the form of their skins, that their 'costumes' are oriented. This means that the furs are not the straightforward utilitarian product of 'ergonomic' principles. It was these non-utilitarian spaces that enabled the construction of the genders to take place. The forms taken by the masculine and the feminine furs were born from something other than mechanical efficiency. What they are wearing is no longer, if it ever was, simply the most efficient form to be had for keeping warm.

Of all the differences in their 'clothing', it is the way in which separate parts of their bodies are clothed and unclothed that is most striking, and most familiar. Each figure could almost be represented diagrammatically with a line marking out the seen and hidden (taboo and non-taboo?) areas of the body. They could be maps of what it is to be masculine or feminine. The male figure has a fur wrap that covers him from the waist almost to his knee. The main task of this 'garment' would appear to be to cover his genitals rather than keeping him warm. The rest of his body is free of any gender marks other than the different hairstyles worn by the two figures and the unlikely ability, on the part of the man, to shave. In contrast the female pelts not only cover much more of the body but are of a more complex construction. The covering begins at knee-level, and proceeds to the upper part of the body and then over the right shoulder. It seems likely that the female 'garment' would require at least two pelts to achieve this sort of covering.

It is not by chance that the artist has staged this little drama of sexual difference within an 'imagined' nuclear family. The picture, as well as imagining for us what Stone Age people wore, also engages with another dimension of the European Imaginary, the story of how sexual difference and reproduction were connected. It is here, where the imagined collective is reproduced both literally and metaphorically, that sexual difference is at its most intense. One thing that the genre of Stone Age pictures helped to dramatise was that they reinforced the Western elites' belief that gender differences had a deep, historical origin. When Europeans looked at these kind of depictions, they saw themselves and their social beliefs present at the first stirrings of 'humanity'. Modesty and its relation to dress are not discussed that much these days and yet, putting to one side the biblical myth of our fall, the patterns of display and covering made by all forms of dress are an important element in the completion of a person. In the picture there is a fur covering the genital area of the male and a 'dress ' for the female that covers the genital area and her breasts. My feeling is that this is not simply a replay of the biblical fall. Undoubtedly, the artist was guided by the patterns of modesty that were current when he drew the picture, but this does not disqualify us from examining how these considerations are played out on the two figures. The dress of both figures focuses on covering the areas concerned with conception and childbirth and the nourishment of infants. The procreative areas of the male and female bodies are covered over but being covered does not eliminate this knowledge of the body of one's opposite sexual partner. A denial of these facts of anatomy by obscuring them with 'furs' appears at its most intense within the baby rearing institution, the nuclear family. Perhaps this is rather like Flugel's idea of dress as a 'compromise formation' but here it both covers and makes visible 'masculinity' and 'femininity'. Once more, there's a lot more taking place with these furs than simply keeping warm.

Masculine and Feminine

'The ladies promptly surrounded him in a glittering garland, bringing with them clouds of every kind of fragrance; one breathed roses, from another wafted springtime and violets, a third was permeated through and through with mignonette. Chichikov just kept raising his nose and sniffing. Their attire reflected a spectrum of their tastes; muslins, satins and cambric of fashionable shades so pale, so very pale that it was impossible even to find names for them (refinement of taste having reached such an extreme). Bows of ribbons and bunches of flowers fluttered here and there on gowns in a most picturesque disorder, although orderly heads had hardly taken great pains over this disorder. An airy headdress barely perched on the rears, and seemed to be saying; 'Oh, I'm going to fly away, I'm only sorry that I can't lift this beautiful lady up with men!' The waists were pulled tight, with contours that were very firm and pleasing to the eye (it must be noted that in general, all the ladies that lived in the town that will remain nameless were rather plump, but laced themselves so artfully and had such pleasant manners that their stoutness escaped all notice) Everything about them had been planned and premeditated with uncommon foresight; their necks and shoulders were exposed precisely as was necessary and no more; each lady bared her possessions to the

point where she felt, according to her own lights, that they were capable
of leading a man to ruin. All the rest was held in reserve with exquisite
taste; either some gossamer-like ribbon or scarf, lighter than the pastry
known as a kiss, ethereally embraced and encircled the neck, or crenulated
battlements of batistes, known as 'modesties', had been allowed to show
from under the neckline of the gown. These modesties, front and back,
concealed that which could no longer lead a man to ruin, but at the same
time compelled him to suspect that it was precisely there that his ruin lay.
Long gloves had not been drawn up to meet the sleeves, but deliberately
left bare the provocative parts of the arms above the elbows, which, for
many of the ladies, breathed an enviable freshness and plumpness. On
some, kid gloves had split from being forced further up the arm. In short,
everything seemed to bear the legend: 'No, this is no province, this is the
national capital, this is Paris itself'.

From *Dead Souls*: Gogol: 1842. Penguin translation: 2004.

Francis Younghusband's Clothing List for the Tibet Expedition of 1903

White shirts (15)
Flannel shirts (12)
Twill shirts (19)
Silk shirts (1)
Coloured stiff shirts (12)
Coloured smooth shirts (8)
Full Dress coat and trousers
Morning coat and grey trousers
Mess coat and waistcoat
Assam silk coat and waistcoat
White evening waistcoat
Light grey suit
Flannel suit
Norfolk breeches

Coats 12 assorted
Headgear
Shikar hat

Thin solar topi
Thick solar topi
Khaki helmet
Forage caps (2)
Brown felt hat
White helmet
White panama

Miscellaneous.
Drawers (28)
Vests (10)
Socks (28)
Collars (32)
Boots and Shoes (18)
Shoe Trees (2)

The Origin of the Origin

As noted elsewhere in this essay, the picture of the Stone Age Family is not just isolated 'back there', it also has connections to the 'here and now' of the picture's artist. (1965) It is on a journey out of a past that is darkness and superstition towards the light and clarity that is our world.

The picture contains recognisable elements such as fire, tools, social relationships and fur 'clothing'. If these things are an earlier version of us then it begs the question as to what sort of a past preceded this scene? What was it that enabled 'advances' such as these to come into being? In short, what is the origin of the fur 'garments' that are depicted as the ancestors of *our* clothing?

At about the same time that the genre scenes of the early life of mankind began to appear in the mid-nineteenth century, a scholarly debate about the origins of clothing started up. This debate lasted well into the 20th century and, after a period of dormancy, it has recently re-emerged but in a somewhat different form. (See Gilligan) The participants fall into two broad groups, each drawing upon different intellectual traditions. Those discussed in this section attempt to explain clothing and body decoration using versions of the theory of natural selection. The other group, discussed in the section titled The Decorators, saw clothing and body decoration as a matter of culture and the social order not biology, or nature.

The Neo-Darwinians

In this section we will look at those explanations that have drawn upon the theory of natural selection and in the section titled *Origin of Origins: The Others* we will look at a group of explanations that argue that the origin of clothing lies within those dimensions of human life called culture.

Darwin's colleague, Alfred Wallace, (1823-1913) — who was often described as being more of a Darwinian than Darwin himself- made a number of observations with regard to clothing. How he understood human clothing (and not, note, bodily decorations in general) was directly related to his belief that the whole of life was ruled by what he called 'The Iron Law of Utility'. As he says 'every aspect of life must now be or once have been useful to the individuals or the races which posses them'. From the brilliance of Amazonian butterflies to the reasons why hen birds are generally dowdier than the cock birds, they are all subject to the iron law of utility. Indeed, for Wallace, utility is the supreme governing principle of all life on earth.

Not content with extending these fundamental ideas into every nook and cranny of the natural world, Wallace set out to explain human societies and the behaviour found in them using a variant of natural selection. According to Wallace, human evolution, and therefore natural selection, appeared to have diverged from its normal pathway. Something had happened within human evolution that made us different to other organisms. What was striking about our bodies was the apparent absence of any clear adaptive features. For instance, we had little body hair in comparison to our simian cousins. Natural selection, in the form of adaptation, appeared to no longer work directly upon the human body. But natural selection was not completely absent from human life. Absent from our bodies, yes, but it was still at work *within* the most distinctive of human 'inventions', culture. Through our accumulation of knowledge and motor skills – something Wallace referred to as Mind- we had created such things as architecture with its ability to build environments that afforded protection. Fire, which gave us the means for cooking and agriculture, which gave us a degree of control over the supply of food and last, but not least, clothing, which, like architecture gave us protection from the elements. Wallace argued that it was the emergence of these *useful* arts that bestowed an advantage on those groups who developed them to the highest degree of efficiency. To understand even such 'non-useful' activities as ritual, art, music, dance, etc, one must first look for the cultural adaptive advantage that was buried in them somewhere. Everything had a use, even the apparently useless. It couldn't exist otherwise. Whilst, at first sight, it might seem that the human intellect was able to override the pressures of natural selection, its logics re-emerged and were played out in the area of culture. Adaptive pressures, and this meant the pressures aiding survival, were displaced onto culture. Clothing was, before everything else, something that's *raison d'être* lay in its usefulness. The furs worn by the inhabitants of the Stone Age family are depicted as being for pure utility in accordance with Wallace's iron law.

The very small number of Neo-Darwinians who have undertaken analyses of human (cultural) appearance have attempted to find an adaptive advantage, buried somewhere within the complexities of human appearance. One of the more promising pathways is the to open up what we look like via Darwin's, still controversial, legacy of sexual selection. This came about as a way of explaining the many non-adaptive bodily features and behaviours that were displayed — usually by the male — leading up to mating. Darwin argued that exceptions to the laws of natural selection had to be made so as to be able to account for these, often, bizarre creatures. It was the male who displayed the most perfect mating features, who was most likely to secure a mate and therefore pass on their genes to the next generation.

A notable, and thought provoking example, is the work done by Camilla Power, on female body painting practices to be found amongst an East African tribe, the Bemba. (11) Power argues that the application of red ochre to their bodies by the women of the tribe can be understood as a form of sexual selection. The red ochre used during rituals, symbolises the blood of menstruation, which in turn is read by the men as evidence that the females are fertile. The females with the most vivid displays are the ones most likely to acquire a mate. No one would argue that appearance and sexual attraction are not bound together in a number of ways. The difficulty is whether something like mate selection (nature) is derived from something so culturally saturated as symbolic markings and gender differences? (Note-Power's study raises some important questions about the line between culture and nature. She seems to be arguing that 'within' cultural forms there are 'cores' of natural and sexual selection. These have infiltrated themselves into cultural forms.)

The most recent which tackles the *origins of clothing* is an interesting piece of controlled speculation undertaken by the anthropologist / archaeologist, Ian Gilligan. I use the word 'speculation' because little direct evidence exists in relation to the birth of clothing. Indeed, it is unlikely that any direct evidence of the earliest forms of clothing, whatever it was will ever be found, making speculation a necessary part of any 'scientific' approach to the problem.

Gilligan's approach draws upon many of the assumptions that Wallace and the Neo-Darwinian tradition held about utility, human ingenuity and efficiency. In a nutshell, Gilligan's argument concerning the appearance of clothing is that it was a *response* on the part of certain human groups who were experiencing climate change in the form of a drop in annual temperatures. As in the picture, it is protection against the cold that is the main reason behind the appearance of clothing. Gilligan argues that this early 'clothing' was made out of animal skins, which were treated and then sewn together to make 'garments'. There is yet another coincidental feature with the picture in as much as it is assumed that these first clothes were made of animal fur. One of the most concrete suggestions he puts forward is that all this took place in Tasmania (There could be other sites) where the environmental conditions were favourable for the 'invention' of clothing. Locating Tasmania, as a likely site for the emergence of clothing is ironic given it was the inhabitants this island, along with the indigenous peoples of Tierra del Fuego and the Andaman Isles that were repeatedly cited by nineteenth and twentieth century anthropologists as going about with little or no 'clothing'. Even as late as 1931, anthropologists were arguing the exact opposite to Gilligan, by claiming that the Tasmanians had 'dispensed' with clothing. (12)

Gilligan's explanation for the emergence of 'clothing' in Tasmania stays within the boundaries of Neo-Darwinian explanations. He makes a clear distinction between clothing and all other bodily adjustments. Clothing belongs to an order of utility that involves a quite different evolutionary pathway to that taken by bodily decoration. The assumption behind this separation is that a 'pure' form of utility can appear divorced from all of the other dimensions of any object made by humans. Clothing must be of some practical use and it is self-evident that clothing acts as a protection against the cold. He stays close to Wallace's assumption that utility lies at the heart of human culture just as it does in the order of nature. Clothing, elementary and otherwise, is a *response* to a thermal prompting from the environment. Its rationality lies in the degree to which it is able to 'solve' this prompting and in so doing it confers an adaptive advantage on the group out of which the response originated. There is an uncanny similarity between Gilligan's notion of animal skin 'clothing' arising as something useful in providing protection against the cold and the furs worn by the inhabitants of the Stone Age family in the depiction.

Wallace's iron law of utility is safe.

The Origin of the Origin: The Decorators

As noted elsewhere in this essay the picture of the Stone Age Family is not just isolated 'back there', it also has connections to the 'here and now' of the picture's artist. (1965) It is on a journey out of a past that is darkness and superstition towards the light and clarity of our world.

The picture contains recognisable elements such as fire, tools, social relationships and fur 'clothing'. If these things are an earlier version of us, then it begs the question as to what sort of a past preceded this scene? What was it that enabled 'advances' such as these to come into being? In short, what is the origin of the fur 'garments' that are depicted as the ancestors of *our* clothing?

At about the same time that the genre scenes of the life of early mankind began to appear in the mid-nineteenth century, there had also started up a scholarly debate about the origins of clothing. This debate was to last well into the 20th century when, after a period of dormancy, it recently re-emerged but in a somewhat different form. (See Gilligan) The participants fell into two broad groups, each drawing upon different intellectual traditions. Those discussed in the *The Neo-Darwinians* section attempt to explain clothing and body decoration using versions of the theory of natural selection. The other group, the one discussed in this section, — *The Decorators* — saw clothing and body decoration as a matter of culture and the social order rather than biology, or nature.

The 'Decorators' debate over the origin of clothes and body decoration begins with Thomas Carlyle's book, *Sartor Resartus.* (13) In it he claims that it was decoration rather than protection (that is clothing as a useful tool) and modesty (The biblical story of the circumstances surrounding the clothing of Adam and Eve) that was the place where clothing originated. To be strictly accurate, it was not the origin of clothing that Carlyle was referring to, rather the first attempts to decorate the body. In laying out protection, modesty and decoration as possible explanations, he set the parameters for the 'origin debate' for the next 130 years. It was Carlyle's deep suspicion of utilitarian rationality that led him to choose decoration as the prime motivation of clothing and body decoration, arguing that, in it, is to be found an embryonic form of spiritual aspiration. Clothing, then, is not just a simple tool or a universal mark of our fallen condition. Clothing, or what passes for clothing at this stage of human development, embodies some of our earliest transcendental longings because in aspiring to what Carlyle calls 'the best', humans must reform, and recast, that most immediate mark of their origin in nature, their physical bodies. Sartorial 'decorations' are seen as a way of displaying the body in a new form. Bodily markings and clothing are an indication of *our* humanity and not the 'humanity' bestowed on us by nature.

For the next one hundred years or more, the debate about the origins of clothing repeatedly found decoration to be the source of clothing and adornment. This is a remarkable consensus given the tight hold that utilitarian ideas and assumptions had on the intellectual elites of Western Europe. (Their influence can be seen at work in the Neo-Darwinian section of this discussion.) A significant exception to both sides of the debate is the political gloss added by Herbert Spencer. (1820-1903) Like

Carlyle, Spencer rejects both the biblical and utilitarian explanations for clothing's origin. Clothing and decoration 'is at first worn from the wish for admiration'. Unlike Carlyle, Spencer draws the story back down to earth and inserts it into the primordial struggle for power. Clothing not only assists at the birth of a system of rank and prestige, it also continues to mark and reinforce the increasingly complex political hierarchies that emerge as society becomes more internally differentiated. Spencer's *ur* garment was really a human skull. Gender power aside no political differentiation, or bodily decoration appears to have infiltrated the Stone—age scene. Politics seems to be absent. (14)

One of the last outings of the debate was in 1930 with the publication of J. C. Flugel's book *The Psychology of Clothes*. (15) Flugel, like so many other contributors to the debate, came out in favour of decoration as the most likely source for clothing but his reasons for doing this, whilst they were fascinating, have largely been ignored by later scholars. According to Flugel, clothes and all our other bodily accoutrements exist because they are 'compromise-formations'. What he means by this is that clothing and bodily decoration are the outcome of a compromise between the demands of functionality and those of aesthetic completion. Neither of these forces can have total control of how we look. As he says:

> 'Art itself (and with it sartorial art) is a compromise between imagination and reality; it deals with real media but implies an inability to find complete satisfaction with reality, and creates a world 'nearer to the heart's desire', away from the limitations and disappointments of reality.
> Flugel: *The Psychology of Clothes,* (16)

Below this aesthetic v functionalism confrontation resides an even more fundamental scene. Flugel argues that the 'adjustments' we make to our bodies are caught between another set of contradictory impulses. The first drive is the desire to display our naked bodies. This is a kind of proto-aesthetic, something that exists prior to the birth of representation. The other is a drive to cover up and so hide our bodies from the gaze, not only of others, but also ourselves. These drive contradict one another and are unable to find full expression. Clothing and bodily decorations come into being as a form of compromise between these two impulses. Clothes both hide, but at the same time are able to draw attention to our bodies through a multitude of embellishments and re-formations. What we can see in the picture, using Flugel as our guide, is a brutal first compromise between an abrupt protective utility which seems to have the advantage over a the creation of a pleasing form, something more likely to emerge as life becomes more less onerous. However, even as he discusses the various strands to the 'origin debate' Flugel seems to sense its exhaustion. He observes that 'we need not here enter into any detailed consideration of this speculative and somewhat arid debate.' There was a space waiting to be filled.

In the late 1950's and the early 1960's, the French critic and intellectual Roland Barthes, published three short essays that, if not caused, then certainly shadowed a complete revolution in how both clothing and fashion were to be regarded. (17) Put bluntly, the old origin debate – which was at death's door anyway – was swept aside and its place was taken by the idea of clothing as a form of communication. At face value there would seem to be nothing revolutionary about such an assertion, something that is self-evident about all forms of bodily adjustments. But it was the rigorous way that Barthes went about establishing his thesis that was to have the most profound influence on later scholars of dress.

Perhaps the most important of his intellectual moves was to ground his notion of clothing as communication by asserting that it was structured like a language. He did this via a sustained critique of the notion of an 'origin' for clothing. The result of this critique was to construe clothing as a radically different entity to the ways it had been shaped within the origin debate. The major characteristics of clothing and, of course body adjustments in general being construed as language are as follows.

He dismisses the search for 'origins' as a waste of time. One is dealing not with a set of objects but rather a system that organises the totality of body adjustments.

Clothing, and the movements it makes as it circulates within the group it belongs to, cannot be derived from the psychology of the individual.

Before anything else, clothing exists as a *meaning*.

The conclusion of this shift to a linguistic model of clothing is that it is not just a collection of disparate objects waiting to be discovered in an archaeological sense, rather, it's essence lies in the fact that it is a structured, language-like system that produces clothing as meaning.

The meanings that clothing and appearance carry are primarily to do with the social make-up of the individual wearing them.

What emerges at the end of this survey of the various theories of clothing's emergence is that the clothing object takes wildly different forms. For Barthes, the materiality of the clothing object is meaningful only as a unit within a much larger ensemble. Flugel's clothing object is a material thing that comes into being to help resolve deep psychological contradictions. Finally, Carlyle sees the marks and shapes of our bodily alterations being an aspiration towards the transcendental.

From these explanations, both the Neo-Darwinian and the Culturalist, it is clear that the one favoured by the Stone Age Family is the response model put forward by Gilligan. What remains to be explained, if we stay within this model, is why, if these are rational responses to a drop in temperature, are the male and female figures dressed differently?

A Last Look

This purpose he (Man) achieves by the modification of external things upon which he impresses the seal of his inner being, and then finds repeated in them his own characteristics. Man does this in order as a free subject to strip the outer world of its stubborn foreignness, and to enjoy in the shape and fashion of things a mere external reality of himself.

G.W.F. Hegel, *Introductory Lectures on Aesthetics*. (18)

In this final look at the Stone Age family, I want to offer the reader a fuller account, albeit a speculative one, of the coming into being of the dressed body. Once again, it must be stressed that 'Dress' or 'dressing' refers to the full range of bodily adjustments that bring about a transformation of the natural human form into a bodily form sanctioned by the prevailing social order. Perhaps the most significant difference between the technological explanation of clothing and the account of dress which I am offering here is that in the latter there is no coming into being of a discrete set of objects called clothing. What one has is a space - the body - and a lexicon of marks and materials that are subsequently applied to the body. Logically I'm not even sure that there is a body upon which 'adjustments' are expended. In all probability the 'body' emerges as the adjustments of dress get made. That is, it comes into being as part of a field of symbolic marks and materials. It adds to, and draws upon, those alternative and imaginary worlds that play such a large role in the life of Homo sapiens.

The explanation of dress I wish to offer here encompasses three dimensions. Social, Form and Imagination.

There are a number of indications that, despite seeming to be isolated from the world around them, the family in the picture is part of a much larger social and cultural unit. Unless the first attempts at bodily transformation through dress were isolated acts of narcissism then what we are searching for must have taken place within a relatively stable, albeit limited, grid of psychological and proto-social relationships. In other words it was collective 'right from the start'.

One recurrent mistake is to make 'social dressing' into a late arrival or an 'ornament', which turns it into something that makes an appearance after, to all intents and purposes, the social is fully formed. Nor should it be seen, because of its supposed late arrival, as something that simply expresses, communicates, or marks something that is already present and is simply waiting for a medium, such as dressing, to become visible. Dress, and bodily adjustments in general, do not just indicate the presence of something that is already there. For instance, dressing is at the heart of establishing gender differences. Dress is constitutive of the social body not simply a medium of its meanings. What we call 'dressing' was, and still is, something that lies at the heart of what it is to be human.

The proto-social impact of dress consists of a set of regulated similarities and differences in which adjustments to the body play a crucial role. The basic building blocks of this form of sociality consists of sorts of dressing that create and make tangible both these similarities and differences. Returning to the question of dressing and gender, we found that whilst both sexes were dressed, they dressed differently and these differences were part of a miniature system of meaning. The types of dress worn by the two or more groups did not come into being independently of each another. A negative dimension, a not-I/not-Us, and a positive affirmation of I/We always accompany acts of bodily transformation, or dressing. If we return to the furs of the mother and father worn by the Stone Age Family there is an affirmation of similarity — even belonging together — in the fact that both were dressed but there is also an assertion of a difference - a not feminine, a not masculine. This play of affirmation and negation can reach extremely complex heights and be embodied in garments, colour, textile, shape, etc. each of which can carry a gender specific charge. Every element of dress is both 'is' and 'is-not'.

Although only just beginning to surface as part of the archaeological repertoire, questions about the *where* and the *when* of human bodily 'adjustments' are already sites of disagreement. What can be said with a degree of certainty is that these bodily concerns seem to be part of a more general set of changes implicated in the emergence of Homo sapiens. It seems that in an increasing number of areas of human behaviour, instinct was no longer playing the dominant role it previously had. Instinct, unmediated nature, or simply what had been given starts to withdraw or is completely absent. Language, more sophisticated toolkits, music, art and in all probability dance could all be seen as cultural responses to the diminution of what, previously, had been guaranteed by the natural order or were activities that had been released by the ebbing away of instinct. I would also place the 'concerns' with the human body amongst these proto-cultural manifestations.

Strictly speaking, in its pre-human condition, there was no form to the body since it was an unconscious given thing. Georges Bataille has described this condition as being ' in the world like water is in water'. (19) As the body emerged from its 'natural' condition, or rather as the naturally given began to recede, the 'body' was transformed into something that was culturally derived not biologically given. Bodily adjustments, those first attempts to endow the body with a form are, therefore, faltering steps on the path of new ways of living that to assume 'responsibility' for the body and the environment (soon to be world) in which it finds itself. But it also marks the moment when, according to the Swiss biologist Adolf Portmann, 'our deficiency in instincts must be seen positively as a special freedom'. (20) That culture 'takes command' means that there is an opening out into a kind of freedom in which new bodily forms, even new worlds can be made.

Endowing the human body with a form would not necessarily have required much labour or much material. A simple mark with red ochre, or shells threaded on string in the form of beads, would have sufficed. What was important was that the form could be both repeated and copied. Repetition gave the body a physical and temporal continuity, both of which are crucial to the identity of the self. Being able to be copied would open up the possibility for relationships and identifications to be cemented between 'like-formed' individuals, the 'we' spoken of earlier.

The emergence of form in those areas of human life no longer given to us by nature enabled humans to install some degree of continuity and predictability into their world. Forms persist, and can rival, even replace nature. The ebbing away of the 'natural' body form is accompanied by a re-forming of ourselves through what we call dressing.

The journey from a simple form of dress to a complex one is part of a broader journey made from elementary groups living to a highly articulated social order. Human collectives are not just 'rational' machines for the satisfaction of material needs, although they certainly do attempt to guarantee that these needs are met. Dress is something that straddles both the mundane dress demands of daily life but at the same time can be a vehicle for realising the metaphysical aspirations of the group. These journeys of transformation, be they routine or the most elevated are never undertaken selectively, or intermittently, by our species. Wherever one encounters (or encountered) human beings – even at the uttermost ends of the earth - they are always dressed. But why should such a condition be universal?

Georges Bataille, in a discussion of the significance of activities such as art, music and eroticism, describes them as places where we can, for the first time, see *human* sensibilities flourishing. Those 'sensibilities' are also, I suspect, sites where the faculty of the imagination starts to be exercised. Despite the fact that many pre-historic archaeologists have stressed the importance for Homo sapiens being able to escape from the mental confines of the here and now, few have made use of a notion of the imagination and to explore what this faculty made possible. Of all the many and various versions of the imagination, the one laid out by the poet S.T. Coleridge still seems to be the one that most carefully maps the movement of the human mind. Its strength is that it is not just a mental activity but also a force that works on the existing, physical environment. As Coleridge puts it, the imagination 'dissolves, diffuses and dissipates' a physical world by breaking it down into fragments, qualities and then reforms, and replays, the fragments, etc into forms that exhibit varying degrees of coherence. It sees the operations of dress as consisting of imagining the body in fresh ways. It takes what is 'lying about' and works this material into socially endorsed figures/bodies.

The 'human sensibilities' mentioned by Bataille are responsible for the production of those objects, images and forms of behaviour which, like their makers, are no longer unmediated products of the natural order. Is not the dressed body also one of these new, 'non-natural' behavioural forms? The imagination (in both its individual and collective form) played, and still plays, a central role in responding to the existential emptiness that opened up with our shift away from the notion of having simply been given. This emptiness was transformed into an imaginative space where endlessly novel bodily forms were, and are, produced. It was the imagination, with its unique ability to both visualise something entirely new, as well being able to enter into the material production of the thing imagined, that placed it at the centre of the activities associated with being dressed.

Perhaps, at last, we are in a position to offer an explanation for the universality of dressing. It is surely connected to the nature of the 'world' that we inhabit since it is a world that, to an ever-greater extent, we have made for ourselves, and that confronts us as the artificial product of human activity. It is not just 'the world' that has to be remade but also the inhabitants of that world, us

Conclusion

The discussion of the Stone Age picture has travelled along two pathways. The first route was to treat the picture as if it were an accurate depiction of 'back then' and so enable an inventory of the figures, their furs and their implements to be compiled. At the same time, the picture has been linked, quite broadly, to the time and place of its origin —1965 and Western Europe. There is, however, a third vantage point that will enable these two viewpoints to be brought together. This is the idea of a 'European Imaginary' that, as this section unfolds, will be seen to be something into which the two different approaches to the depiction can be incorporated. It should be remembered that despite their, at times, ridiculous appearance, the figures were the first secular version of how our clothing came into being. Adam and Eve are nowhere to be found.

What the 'European Imaginary' means in this instance, is the collective imagination that circulated amongst European populations between the middle of the 19th and most of the 20th century. It is here that the picture of the Stone Age Family lives and breathes. The European Imaginary was the crucible wherein the scant evidence being thrown up by archaeology of European pre-history was knitted together into visual tableau. It was only in the second half of the 19th century that tentative glimpses into the lives of 'prehistoric man' got under way. This dearth of evidence provided fruitful territory for the operations of the Imaginary as it threaded the scant evidence into a coherent picture of life 'back then'. It is not by chance that some of the first places where pictorial representations of early man could be seen were in museums.

Despite the absence of any direct evidence, Prehistoric people were, right from the outset depicted wearing animal furs. What emerged from these first attempts to represent early humans was a limited, but resilient, visual genre, one that first surfaced in oil painting and scientific illustrations; museum exhibits and then spread to popular culture in such forms as film, comics, TV (*The Flintstones*) and animated cartoons. The visual supposition behind all of these depictions is that it was animal fur that was used in the first man-made garments and that they were used as protection against the cold. In addition to this 'factual' supposition about animal fur, there is the further implication that the Stone Age people were our ancestors and so their furs were *our* first bodily coverings and the ancestors of contemporary garments. The European Imaginary is the place and the process whereby 'back there' is put into a relation of mutuality with 'here and now'. When we look at the picture of the Stone Age family we are looking at early versions of ourselves navigating that crucial moment when 'clothing' first appeared. Their clothes are our clothes; our clothes are their clothes.

What the pictures does is to make visible that part of the European Imaginary that is concerned with where 'we' came from and it does this by showing the people of the Stone Age at a crucial moment in their evolution — wearing animal furs.

If these images render the collective visible to itself what sort of a picture is it drawing of prehistoric people? To answer this we have to return to the question that was posed at the beginning of this investigation, 'Why fur?' The Imaginary holds together two aspects of the use of fur. It points to where the fur wearers have come from as well as indicating where they are headed. What these Stone Age pictures are doing is to show early humans at the instant when the 'invention' of fur garments takes place and so propels them out of animal-hood. (It is always an invention that is useful.) Or, like our family in the illustration, they are depicted in a 'furred' condition soon after the appropriation of animal skins as protection against the cold.

It was the act of killing, skinning and wearing furs, which indicated that early people had moved beyond the condition of the animals and were heading towards a fully 'clothed' future. In both instances the pictures rehearse those crucial moments when Homo sapiens took some steps towards who they were to become. We know that this imaginary drama of dress had profound implications for those who believed in it. Beyond 'our' ancestors were people who never became 'clothed'. These are the people that Europeans would described as 'naked except for....' And ' naked but for....' No clothes no moral affinity.

At the beginning of this section I suggested that pictures such as the one we have been studying were amongst the first to present Europeans with a secular account of the life of their ancestors. What it shows is that the embryonic 'clothing', namely the animal furs, were the product of human ingenuity, and need, rather than a supernatural intervention. No God provided us with clothing despite the proximity of the furs in the picture to those gratefully worn by Adam and Eve. ('Unto Adam and to his wife did the Lord God make coats of skins, and clothed them.') There are a number of implications that flow from this secular 'origin' of clothing. As the given body ebbed away there was no automatic replacement body to take its place. It was 'us' that had to create the body anew, to remake it, because there was no pre-ordained shape, or form, for us to become. The world is indifferent to our presence and so we have to make a world (in which we need to include our body) where we do have some degree of significance. We do this by adding to, or replacing it with, our own versions of ourselves.

Postscript

Having finally reached the end of this examination of the Stone Age family and their furs one last thing needs to be considered. The date of the illustration is 1965, so almost fifty years have elapsed since it was first published. Depictions like the one we have been engaged with do not persist undiminished. The place they come from will certainly change, and its view of itself can undergo some drastic refurbishments. There is a lifetime to these 'scenes', just as there is a lifetime to the groups, or civilization, of which they are part. At its broadest reach the genre of stone age scenes was one of a number of places where time, place, intellectual content, even food and drink marks out where being European peters out, but also of course, where being European begins. The fate of the *Stone Age* tableau is not so clear-cut as other European boundary markers. Race looked as if it was fading, but has recently undergone a revival using religion as a supplementary marker for race. As a coherent *image* it seems to have faded away, and may now only linger in the dustier museum displays or in less up-to-date children's books. Despite the diminished clarity of its image it is still capable of organising the 'evidence' into a familiar form:

Humans draped in furs.

Notes and References

(1) Ian Gilligan, 'Clothing and modern human behaviour: prehistoric Tasmania as a case study', in *Archaeology in Oceania*, December 2007.

(2) Barber, E. W., *Women's Work: The First 20,000 Years: Women, Cloth and Society in Early Times*, 1994.

(3) Marian Vanhaeren in, Eric A. Powell, 'In Style in the Stone Age', *Archaeology*, 2013 and Interview with Marian Vanhaeren, 'More Than Ornament' in *Archaeology*, 2006.

(4) Vanhaeren, ibid.

(5) Charles Darwin, *The Descent of Man*, Penguin, 2004, p.689.

(6) T. Ingold (ed), *What is an Animal?* Unwin Hyman, 1988, pp.77-83.

(7) Gilligan, ibid.

(8) Adrian Desmond and James Moore, *Darwin*, London, 1991, pp.132-140.

(9) Chapman, Anne, 'The Great Ceremonies of the Selk'nam and the Yamana' in

McEwan, Colin, Borrero, Luis A. and Prieto, Alfredo in McEwan, Borrero, and Alfredo (eds) *Patagonia: Natural History, Prehistory and Ethnography at the Uttermost End of the Earth*, British Museum Press, 1997, pp. 82-109.

(10) Susan Sontag, *Against Interpretation*, New York, 1961, p. 36.

(11) Camilla Power, ' 'Beauty Magic' The Origins of Art', in Robin Dunbar, Chris Knight, and Camilla Power, *The Evolution of Culture*, Rutgers U. P. 2003, pp. 92-112.

(12) V.F. Calverton (ed.) *The Making of Man: an Outline of Anthropology*, The Modern Library, 1931.

(13) Thomas Carlyle, *Sartor Resartus*, University of California Press, 2000.

(14) Michael Carter, 'Herbert Spencer's Sartorial Protestantism' in Michael Carter, *Fashion Classics: From Carlyle to Barthes*, Berg, 2003, pp. 19- 40.

(15) J. C. Flugel, *The Psychology of Clothes*, Hogarth Press, 1971 edition.

(16) J. C. Flugel, *The Psychology of Clothes*, p. 237.

(17) See part 1, "Clothing History' in Roland Barthes, *The Language of Fashion*, Berg, 2006.

(18) G. W.F Hegel, *Introductory Lectures on Aesthetics*, ed. Michael Inwood, Penguin, 1993.

(19) Georges Bataille, *Theory of Religion*, Zone Books, New York, 1992, p. 23.

(20) See Adolf Portmann, *Animal Forms and Patterns: A Study of the Appearance of Animals*, Faber, London, 1952.

Chapter Five

Formality and Informality
in (Mainly) Men's Dress

Fashion scholar, Efrat Tseelon, has suggested that it is time for us to relinquish the categories of formality and informality. As she says, these are '... fundamental categories that run... through much theory and practice of the field of fashion'. She continues, ':

> 'the distinction between formality and informality [is] — perhaps the last remaining bastion of stereotypical thinking.' ' (1)

It is not immediately clear what Tseelon means by 'stereotypical thinking', but, if we leave to one side the minor nuances, one theme does become clear and that is redundancy. To designate something 'stereotypical thinking' is to suggest that the linguistic categories of formality and informality have lost touch with the empirical reality they are supposed to engage with. A gap has opened up between the category and its object, and into this gap stereotypes are able to take up residence. The work undertaken by such stereotypes creates a synthetic coherence that is largely, but not wholly, indifferent to the empirical diversity of clothing's forms, styles and contexts. Stereotypical thinking, in this context, is largely devoted to naming rather than describing. Stereotypes, and the thinking associated with them, can produce a range of figures — something like a cast of characters — that is ideologically, and therefore politically, inspired. It may seem that these collective images are describing their object but in reality their task is to pass moral and political judgments on the clothing and the individuals wearing it.

The realms of clothing and dress are filled with such sartorial judgments, and 'true' stereotypical thinking simply reproduces this pre-digested stock of characters rather than registers the actual make-up of a designated empirical reality. I want to engage with Tseelon's assertion that formality and informality are nothing more than a set of exhausted labels, not by revivifying them through the importation of external signs but by drawing out something already in their constitution. Running beneath formality, formal, informality and informal is the aesthetic category of 'form', and form can provide a direct route into the central role played by aesthetics in the organisation of formal(ity) and informal(ity). It is only if formal and informal can be shown to no longer contain what might be called content that they can be regarded as redundant. It is through the lens of aesthetics that I hope to show that the categories retain considerable descriptive power and are capable of engaging accurately with the contours of an empirical reality.

Another important feature of formal(ity) and informal(ity) is the way in which they are frequently cited as a pair: the mention of one seems to call into being the other. This dual recitation contains much more than an innocent enumeration of separate and independent entities. At first glance, the relationship between formal and informal might appear simply oppositional, but beneath is a relationship of mutual dependence. Formal clothing is not the buttoned-up dress that it is so often assumed to be, nor is informal dress simply an absence of formality. The formal can carry traces of informality while the informal can take the form it does to the extent it rejects the principles of formal dress, thereby granting the formal a degree of recognition. The categories of formal(ity) and informal(ity) are more than simply ways of describing the clothing of certain dress genres, although they undoubtedly do this; they also register something of the relationship that exists between them. A small but telling example will make the nature of this mutual dependence clear.

To complete the classic male outfit of a suit, collared shirt, tie and brogues or oxfords, a handkerchief in the breast pocket of the jacket is considered essential. While there is agreement that the handkerchief should be coloured (but without figurative motifs) there is a measure of disagreement about how it should be arranged in the pocket. One school maintains that it should display a geometric outline above the top of the pocket, a dubious move that has led to the wearing of a 'false' handkerchief made of paper. Another school of thought, and a strategy that seems favoured by etiquette books on male dressing, prefers the handkerchief pushed into the breast pocket with a random expanse of fabric left showing. (2) This latter style appears to welcome the presence of informality, the handkerchief contrasting with the formal principles otherwise governing the male outfit. The exposed portion of the handkerchief exhibits certain features of informality, such as uncontrollability, formlessness and unpredictability. Each time the handkerchief is placed in the pocket a new configuration is produced, and there is none of the constancy of form that is such a feature of the outfit.

Formal(ity) and informal(ity) appear to be some distance from the hollow labels typical of Tseelon's 'stereotypical thinking'. What follows is a deliberately restricted exploration of these two orders of dress to see if they retain any content over and above that supplied by a pair of exhausted and redundant categories. I want to start with an examination of ironing, especially the ironing of clothes.

Ironing

[This exploration of ironing is based on my experience in a domestic situation. It has to be acknowledged that the range of garments thought to require ironing has narrowed, while personal experience of ironing has shrunk due to a greater use of commercial outlets.

Despite this attenuation, the desire for certain clothes to be in an ironed state remains just as strong.]

Of all the techniques we bring to bear on our clothes, ironing is perhaps the most resistant to understanding. As might be expected, the literature dealing with it is almost non-existent, apart from some perfunctory historical reviews. (3)

The mundane nature of ironing and its position within the domestic routine - self-evident and mute- has meant that it has elided any sort of sustained scrutiny. Why would anyone bother to try and understand such a trivial activity? While the physics of ironing are well understood, the 'point' of it remains hazy and abbreviated. There are, however, some features associated with it that suggest the presence of dimensions not normally registered by simple, practical explanations of this activity. What is remarkable is that something so insignificant forcefully insists that we attend to its demands. Whether it is the desire to iron, and so render smooth the garments one is aiming to wear, or the feeling of vulnerability that can arise from its absence, ironing seems to be an integral part of our relationship to clothing. This suggests something more than an insignificant and commonplace activity. As for many other household tasks, such as tidying-up and cleaning, both of which have myriad non-practical dimensions, there is a code of silence surrounding ironing. It is not even assigned a clear utilitarian purpose, regarded as just another self-evident task that must be done. That said, there are some tangible physical and aesthetic pleasures to be had from the activity of ironing, the chief of which is the successful preparation of clothes for wearing. The questions that need to be asked are: What is it that ironing does? What is the nature of preparation performed by ironing? And what difference is there between the pre- and post-ironed condition of our clothes?

The situation in which domestic ironing usually takes place has a number of components. (Commercial laundries use a different pressing technology. In place of the hand irons, stand-up steam irons are used. Instead of weight and pressure, commercial irons rely on the application of heat and steam.) There will be, of course, the ironer, who may be adept, or not, at the task; despite appearances, good ironing is a skill not an instinctual activity. There must be an iron capable of generating sufficient heat to eliminate unwanted creases, as well as to install a certain number of creases to block out the garment's shape. The ironing board, or a flat surface of some kind is essential for the success of ironing. This flat surface in combination with the iron guarantees the smooth, or pressed, condition of the clothes. In all probability there will be a basket of un-ironed clothes, waiting to be pressed, and another basket or designated place where ironed garments will be held until they are put away. The task at hand is to convert the un-ironed clothing into the ironed clothing, and at the same time provide an answer to the question: What is it that ironing does?

It is easy to see the practical consequences of ironing. On the one hand, it eliminates the chaotic pattern of creases that results from washing and drying, replacing these creased areas with smooth surfaces. But on the other hand, as already mentioned, the ironer may use the iron to contradict this process of 'de-creasing' by impressing a number of sharp creases — creases that are often edges — onto the garment. It is out of these sharply delineated edges that the shape of the garment will emerge. So ironing works with two aims in mind: the elimination of the unwanted and the imparting of the desired. This much is certain, but what do these smooth surfaces and sharp edges mean?

There is a degree of anecdotal unanimity as to what the true purpose of ironing is. Most are variations on a belief that the aim and result of ironing clothes is to make them new again, or at least to appear as new. Which leads to the questions: What is the nature of the new? And how does ironing participate in its creation? While they did not discuss ironing directly, Thorstein Veblen and Georg Simmel are two scholars with some pertinent things to say about the new and its relationship to clothing. (4)

Veblen divided the social order into two very different ways of living. On the one hand there was the portion of society that was dominated by certain 'high' values, which he ironically referred to as the 'honorific'. On the other was the remainder of the population, which he characterised as the 'producers'. This latter group engaged in useful physical labour; its members could be summed up as useful people leading useful lives. Their clothing was likewise functional. It indicated nothing more than that it is, and has been, worn. No stigma attached to the marks left by wearing and work. Unfortunately, in a society where the values of the 'honorific' are dominant, no value other than negative value can accrue to producers. Nothing could be more different than the values and behaviour of the group that lived by the rules of the honorific. Theirs was a way of life in which all signs of useful labour had been eliminated, and where constant effort was needed to keep them at bay. To maintain one's membership of what Veblen called the 'leisure class', one had to be able to constantly display one's ability to pay. Veblen referred to this as 'pecuniary strength'. One way of doing this was to regularly deploy new things as a sign of one's purchasing power. An excellent way to demonstrate pecuniary strength was to always appear in new clothes, or clothes that appeared to be new. In keeping with the laws of the honorific realm, new clothes were those in which the signs of wear and tear (physical labour and shortage of money) were absent.

If we extrapolate Veblen's ideas to ironing, it becomes an activity that eliminates signs that the garment has had previous outings, in particular the creases that result from washing; it restores the major edges that give the garment shape. If ironing restores and maintains the 'newness' of clothing, then in Veblen's terms it is part of an economic strategy to accumulate prestige on behalf of the wearer. Ironing, then, is a (mild) striving for the honorific.

Georg Simmel's approach to the sartorial 'new' was rather different from that of Veblen. His concern was with the aesthetic consequences that wear and tear has on our clothing, rather than with the socio-economic foundations to our love of the new. Simmel argued that the longer a garment was worn the more it would carry the personal imprint of its wearer. The individual shape and particular movements of the wearer would be imprinted on the garment, giving it a quite distinct set of features. It was precisely this mounting presence of the personal that rendered the garment 'not new'. For Simmel, a garment's newness is in the form it has before it descends into a worn, and therefore personal, condition. Simmel's form of the new is more than a material entity, although it manifests itself in a material form. It is also a philosophical form, something above and beyond the individual and so independent of each single act of sustained wearing. Lodged in Simmel's conception of the 'true' forms of our clothing is an idea that the form of the new is at the same time an ideal. The new form of a garment is a condition where it is both complete and beyond the predations wear and tear. The place of this form of newness is not singular; it can appear in fashion photography, department store dummies, fashion illustration, fashion shows etc. However, among the living, this form of newness may only appear briefly before entropy sets in. This is why it can so often be found in visual representations rather than among the living. The former are more malleable and they don't age with use. What the realm of the ideal presents us with, and what makes it so attractive, is that it is a place where our garments are forever new, with all the existential implications that carries.

Extrapolating from Simmel's ideas about the nature of the personal and the new, ironing may now be seen as an activity that liberates the garment from a close attachment to its wearer. It erases all traces of the personal that have undermined its status as an ideal. Ironing is a renewal of a garment's pristine form, and this investment liberates clothing from its life in the particular and reintroduces it to the realm of the general. The garment, if ironing is successful, rests in a state of formal completion. It is new again, or at least closer to new than it was before it was smoothed out.

Both Veblen and Simmel provide powerful explanations of the new in relation to clothing. Following Veblen, we would have to agree that we iron our clothes in preparation for some kind of public appearance and the inevitable scrutiny that goes with it. But Veblen's conception of sartorial dilapidation seems limited. At its heart is the presence of marks upon the surface of garments, marks that are indicators of 'unworthy' activity. But what of the remainder of the garment upon which these signs of wear and tear are inscribed, the dimension of the garment called its shape or form? Simmel's notion of an ideal form gradually disintegrating into the personal and the particular seems far more inclusive than Veblen's construal of the agents of destruction that undermine clothing's newness. Ironing is a restoration of form, an aspiration towards the ideal, and that ideal is manifest right across the clothing spectacle, the place where clothes are worn but never display any signs of wear.

For one last time I want to revisit the domestic situation in which ironing takes place. In the list of ironing's components there is a set of garments not yet mentioned. This set comprises garments intentionally left un-ironed. These garments retain their creases, indeed they are the very opposite of ironed garments. The adjectives thought appropriate to ironed clothes, such as 'smart', 'neat' and 'tidy', are generally not applied to un-ironed clothes. There may be a lack of sharp edges for the iron to follow and emphasise; there may be no well-defined outline or shape for the passage of the iron to restore. Indeed, these garments can exhibit a marked patina of wear and tear, and they can revel in accommodating themselves to the body and the movements of the wearer. Inside this aesthetic of un-ironed informality there is no place for sartorial newness and formal completion. Indeed, in many ways these characteristics of the new are being refused.

My first encounter with Levi's jeans took place in 1963. I had no previous knowledge of them and was even unaware that they were American in origin. But when I pulled on that first pair I also took onboard a set of rules governing how they should be worn. I can't ever remember being aware of these rules, other than as subconscious imperatives. Chief among this etiquette was that they should never be ironed. At the time I had no idea why ironing was forbidden, I simply obeyed the rule. It was only years later, with the increased popularity of Levi's and when the exceedingly uncool leg-crease look made an appearance, that the past began to make sense. Like a post-dated cheque, I, at last, knew that the un-ironed condition of my first pair of Levi's had been an unanswerable blow against that most domesticated of activities, ironing.

For and Against

The categories formal and informal are not just names given to two independent sets of clothing. As noted earlier, these categories are not independent of one another, nor are they simply ways of indicating a straightforward difference between them. Formal and informal are bound together in a complex relationship of mutuality and opposition. It is the nature of this relationship that I will investigate in this section, in particular what this relationship can reveal about the forms and styles assumed by the two orders of clothing.

The relationship between formality and informality in dress is currently (in 2012) played out on Sydney television screens. Without warning, male presenters in a limited number of contexts have stopped wearing ties, even though they continue dress in suits and business shirts. The collar is never worn out of the jacket, nor is it worn raised, à la James Dean. If it were, it would appear a considered casual style. Tieless and with the collar worn inside the jacket carries the feeling of spontaneous gesture. Tieless appearances are confined largely to morning television; although there is some evidence that 'tielessness' is migrating to news commentary programs and to talk shows. Live appearances in the evening are almost always conducted wearing ties. Ties are certainly required for the evening news but not for the morning breakfast shows; formality, it would seem, appears as the sun goes down.

So what is happening here? The informality of male television presenters results from the mechanical insertion of a non-formal element into the classic male dress of a suit, collared shirt, tie etc. Garish bowties and lurid waistcoats are signs of bad taste, even eccentricity, but not of informality. The informal emerges, and is played out, within the garments and principles of male formal dress so that removing one's tie is a translated gesture, a gesture of informality translated into the language of the male suit. Informality, in this instance, is signalled more by the absence of a particular item than by its presence, and, this kind of adjustment to one's dress is a much-favoured route into the informal. But more of this interplay between formality and informality remains to be uncovered. The removal of the necktie is not a random gesture. It is a translation of perhaps the single most common principle of male informality — drastic simplification of one's neckwear — something undertaken in the name of comfort or, more likely, as a gesture of personal liberation. With regards to male television presenters, what seems to be happening is a departure from the rules of male formal dress, that is achieved, either by removing an item of clothing (the tie) or by adjusting one's dress in certain sanctioned ways, such as removing one's jacket and/or rolling up one's shirtsleeves. Each alteration constitutes a break away from the sanctioned forms and rules of male dressing. But, just as this break is *not* the product of a random gesture, nor is it a leap into an unstructured void. It is a journey towards informality, an existential condition that is best embodied in revisions to formal dress. Being without a tie is not just a sign of informality, it is informality itself. In the case we have been examining, the formal draws upon the sartorial repertoire of the informal, translating what it borrows into the language of the suit, shirt, tie etc. This simple-looking gesture of removing one's tie encompasses both a moving *away from* as well as a *moving towards*. Formal and informal dress are bound to each other by a structure of affirmation and negation, a structure that enables a garment or a whole outfit to establish both what it is and what it is not. Removing one's tie is both a partial negation of the formal rules of male dress and an affirmation of the relaxed, tieless state that is the informal. But, nevertheless, this 'relaxation' takes place within a set of formal dress principles that are negations of informal modes of dress.

The presence of this dual declaration within clothing confirms the more general claim that garments and clothing genres are not isolated, autonomous entities. They are always joined, through a network of relationships, to the clothing worlds that surround them. One such relationship is in the exchanges that take place between the orders of formal and informal dress. Here, an item of clothing, or a whole outfit, opens itself to its opposite category, which is likewise in an 'open' condition. It is the presence of this mutual breach that enables traffic between the two orders to take place. More specifically, the forms, styles and gestures that are the building blocks of sartorial formality and informality are organised into declarations of affirmation and/or negation. Dress does not consist of objects that are expressions of a unitary essence. These objects are the result of being both *engaged by* and *engaged with* other orders of clothing.

One place where the play of negation and affirmation is especially clear is in the long-standing antagonism between what, following Elizabeth

Wilson, I call Bohemian dress and the more conventional modes of male dress epitomised by the suit, collared shirt, tie etc. (5) It is neither possible nor appropriate to present a detailed account of this long and complex 200-year-old quarrel. It was an enmity that surfaced in all major cities of Europe and North America, and as well as in sartorial differences it was manifest in aesthetic disputes, contrary political allegiances and even geographical separation. The affirmation and negation of the two orders of dress was played out — according to which side one was on — as a drama of liberation from constraint and conformity. Bohemian dress became an important element in the wearer's pursuit of freedom and personal authenticity. Dress would no longer be an alienating practice but would be drawn closer to the true wishes of the heart. From the side of 'conventionality', Bohemian dress was interpreted as evidence of moral degeneration, something dangerously anti-social, politically charged and, if all else failed, unhygienic. Within the borders of this dispute, the play of affirmation and negation drew upon the whole appearance of each party. Single garments, colours, textiles and shapes, not to mention hairstyles and footwear, were all counters in the judgments thrown by each side at its opposite number. An excellent example of affirmation and negation as it relates to footwear can be found in the opening passages of Tom Wolfe's *Kandy-Kolored Tangerine-Flake Streamline Baby*, where he contrasts the shoes worn by the 'heads' with those worn by the FBI agents, who have them under surveillance:

> The heads have a thing about shoes. The worst are shiny black shoes with shoelaces in them. The hierarchy ascends from there, although practically all low-cut shoes are unhip, from there on up to the boots heads like light, fanciful boots, English boots of mod variety, if that is all they can get, but better something like hand-tooled Mexican boots with Caliente Dude Triple A toes on them. So see the FBI-black-shiny-laced-up FBI shoes …'
> (6)

John Wilkes was a radical Whig journalist, political activist and rake, who lived and worked in London in the 18th century. In the second half of the century he began to gain a reputation as an impassioned public speaker whose appearance at these gatherings drew comments from fellow journalists. Wilkes, along with his fellow radicals, often left off wearing wigs, and some grew their hair in styles that looked both wild and dishevelled. They began to unravel their elaborate neck cloths, 'forgot' to keep their clothes clean and, in a move full of prescience, adopted carefully selected items of lower-class clothing. Wilkes's appearance, when he spoke in public, was often described as 'neglectful', as if he had just that minute torn himself away from some all-absorbing activity that had caused him to forget the rules of public dress. Dress and appearance were trifles compared to the important matters with which he was at that moment engaged. What was different about Wilkes's appearance was that he wasn't wearing the sanctioned clothing of informality available to a person of his class; instead, his 'neglectfulness' of dress, his novel type of informality, took the form of breaking the rules of formal attire. At the heart of Wilkes's strategy, albeit in an embryonic form, was a sense that a new and more authentic way of being (and this, of course, included appearance) lay in territory beyond the conventional. The nature of that territory was indicated by the violation of formal dress codes. Richard Sennett has described Wilkes and the city he lived in, London, as 'overturning the principles of appearance of the *ancien regime*'. (7) What had started out as a sartorial strategy of a small group of prominent individuals became a democratic ploy open to all: 'Babette, dishevelled, has the careless dignity of someone too preoccupied with serious matters to know or care what she looks like.' (8)

In 1905, Welsh artist Augustus John and his wife, Dorelia, purchased a Romany caravan and set off with their children to lead the travelling life. The full story of their adventures cannot be told here but the ways in which they dressed while on the road reveal a great deal about the attitude that underwrote the adventure. Both had become enamoured of the Romany life, and by adopting Romany dress they imagined they could enter into the spirit of the travelling people they had met on an earlier occasion. Augustus dressed in loose-fitting trousers and a baggy shirt, which he wore outside his trousers. He wore neither tie, of course, nor any other complicated neck machinery. Socks were banished, and on his feet he wore sandals. To top it all, his hair and his beard were worn in a wild, 'negligent' manner. What had been a sartorial interval with Wilkes was, with Augustus John, a semi-permanent way of dressing. Dorelia redesigned her dress along the same lines. She abandoned her corset and wore 'peasant-style' dresses stripped of the ornamentation so popular among women of the Edwardian era. On her head she wore a scarf, the antithesis of the jumbo-sized hats in fashion at the time. Like Augustus, she wore sandals. While Augustus modulated his dress in later life, Dorelia maintained this style for the rest of her days.

The dress of Wilkes emerges out of formal wear; it was an adjustment of formal wear. The dress of Augustus and Dorelia, in contrast, consists of garments independently assembled as negations of formal dress and as affirmations of freedom. The garments are 'in touch' with formal wear as its negation, not as direct adjustments to the garments of formal wear. The dress of Augustus and Dorelia shared a common set of negating and affirming principles. What they wore was part of a broader *homage* to the Romany life, a life they imagined to be freer and more authentic than the one offered by conventional society. 'Authenticity' is not a word that describes the wearing of conventional male attire. Correct, or appropriate maybe, but not authentic. What they wore was both a rejection of conventional clothes — and the conventional way of life upon which they rested — and a way for them to demonstrate their admiration for the Romany life they so admired. Every element of their dress was both an 'is' and a 'not that' — an affirmation and a negation.

Form, Formal and Formality

What is it that presents itself as formal in those exemplars of men's formal dress, the Suit and Black tie? In part, the answer rests in the way they are able to persist, apparently unchanged, for extended periods of time. The codification of the broad outlines of these outfits together with the way in which control is exercised over a number of permitted variations marks them off from non-formal clothing genres, in which variations tend to be the result of individual choice. Those enamoured with male formal wear often point to its 'timeless' quality, something that has enabled it to rise above the fluctuations of fashion. This stability is thought to constitute the superiority of this clothing. Using a version of Darwinian natural selection, it is argued that formal wear has remained the same because it is best adapted to its task. Somehow this stylistic persistence (which is, in itself, debatable) acquires moral associations. But as I hope to show, this duration of formal wear is not simply the result of stable but arbitrary physical arrangement. The formality rests upon a marriage between sartorial regulation and aesthetic structure.

Two sorts of male dress are under consideration here. The first consists of the suit (three-piece or two-piece), tie, collared shirt and formal shoes. The second is the Dinner suit, or Black tie, described by Robin Dutt as consisting of 'basically, a black suit' together with a 'black tie... which should only and ever be black' and 'a shirt that is always white'. 9 These are the foundations upon which a greater or lesser degree of personal variation is permitted. In this section I want to examine how rule and aesthetics combine to create the formal and formality. The section will end by looking at a number of places and situations in which what appears to be a collective and personal urge towards form spills out from the body and its sartorial envelopes, moving into the world around it.

Form

The overt presence of form in both the formal and formality — and, in a different way, in the informal — indicates the fundamental role it plays in the constitution of the Suit and Black tie. At its most general, form can be thought of as a particular arrangement of physical materials, and it is the specific qualities of this arrangement that invests dress with its material identity. This arrangement attains the status of true form from the degree to which it is stable and it persists. In addition, the rules for correctly dressing in the Suit or Black tie are shared among the population at large. These are rules that are collectively held, and as such they are repeated and renewed each time dressing takes place.

Form, then, is a specific arrangement of physical material produced by human activity. Because of this human ingredient, form, as we are describing it here, resides in the realm of culture. It is not something that originates in the natural order. To dress or be dressed — and therefore to form him or her anew — commences with the erasure of their given physical form. Dressing is a transformation, or better a translation, of the wearer's bodily flesh into the materials, shapes and colours out of which the forms of dress are made. In the case of the Suit and Black tie, the body is re-formed and translated in such a way that it appears to be composed of wool, cotton, silk and leather deployed according to the principles of formal attire.

Form, however, entails more than an arrangement of physical 'stuff' in a distinctive manner. As has already been suggested, it is only fully present if the arrangement is able to achieve some degree of stability and persistence. It is the presence of these two components that maintain the identity and integrity of a particular garment or set of clothes. Form is not only responsible for initiating the distinctive qualities of an item of dress; it also works to ensure the integrity of the outfit, or garment, is protected. This is done by controlling the degree of variability allowed to play across a specific set of clothes — in this case the Suit and Black tie — enabling the outfit's identity to be maintained without resorting to the imposition of brute uniformity. This 'controlled' variation can be seen in the collared shirt worn as part of a Suit. While the presence of a collared shirt is compulsory, the collar is allowed a degree of variability. It may vary in shape: pointed or rounded. It may vary from standard white through a range of pastel shades (dark shades are frowned upon, as are patterns). It may vary in how it is attached to the body of the shirt: free or button-down. The suit too has a number of points of variation: turn-ups, no turn-ups; two or three buttons on the jacket; and the number of vents in the jacket. Above and beyond these features are the differences in the cut and look of the Suit as a whole. The degree of formality that governs Black tie is considerably more intense than that of the Suit. The colour code of black and white must be strictly adhered to. Collar shapes and attachments have varied over time, but these seem to follow dictates of slow-moving fashion rather than the Suit variations that result from personal inclination.

These points of variability are played out against a backdrop of 'proper' dressing. Even where a degree of variation is permitted, there will be a 'gold standard' of how to dress correctly. In the case of the Suit, multiple variations are allowed, and yet the integrity of the whole remains. The rules governing Black tie are impatient with variation and elevate uniformity to a paramount position. If one of the effects of uniformity is the creation of an homogenous presence, the strict dress code of Black tie takes its wearers to the very limits of voluntary 'civilian' dress.

Formality: The Rules of Dressing

A number of difficulties emerge from the definition of form used so far. A literal reading might suggest all types of 'forming' result in the creation of all things 'formal'. This would mean every item of clothing had the right to be called formal, as all possess form in one way or another. This view is considerably broader in reach than that associated with its more common usage, in which formal refers to a limited set of garments held together by a particular set of dress principles. This type of male dress, in the form of the Suit and Black tie, is governed by the limited sense of formal dealt with here.

One could characterise the formal and formality as the place where form materialises and acquires an identity, an identity that comprises two dimensions. There are rules and conventions that govern *what* and *how* certain clothes are to be worn. Accompanying these rules is a set of aesthetic principles, the task of which is to provide formality with a look. It does this by creating a visual analogue for the formal integration of the outfit and its sartorial completion. Formality binds rule and garment together into a meaningful unit. But if we bear in mind the earlier discussion of the ways in which dress is engaged in a process of affirmation and negation, this power to determine what garments are accorded the status of formal is as much about what cannot or should not be worn as it is about what can be worn. It establishes what garments do not fit with the principles of formality and rejects them on the grounds of aesthetic inappropriateness. It would be, for instance, unthinkable to wear trainers with Black tie.

Perhaps the most important and distinctive rule is the way in which these outfits are approached as unified, integrated wholes. Integration in this context means the making of an harmonious whole by combining separate parts. Even their names, the Suit and the Dinner suit (the alternative to Black tie), refer to the totality of the outfit, rather than to its parts. Every aspect of a formal outfit, from the colour of the shoes to the style of the necktie, is subject to a single, unifying regime. These controls mean that little, or nothing, may be added or taken away from the ensemble. The variations that are permitted are both limited and strictly controlled so as not to violate the general aesthetic principles of sartorial completion. While it is possible for some garments to migrate to less formal contexts, for example, the tie and shirt, the ready availability of men's casual wear has made such migration less and less inviting. One exception is the way male politicians, both in Australia and America, signal their informality by wearing a neatly pressed white business shirt with denim jeans. I'm not sure whether it is the shirt or the jeans that appear uncomfortable. Historically, it was an absence of casual wear for men that made informal adjustments of the Suit the only possible way into the informal.

The greater the integration of the formal outfit, the less likely it is that individual garments will be detached from their regulatory and aesthetic milieu. So while it is possible for the Suit to be 'punctured' by elements of the informal, no such possibility is open to the Black tie. It has only one way of being worn and that is with total formality at all times. An exception to this, however, was a stage gesture favoured by American male crooners of the 1940s and 50s. They would unbutton their jackets and loosen their bowties, which would then hang loose. This often signified a move away from the delivery of a quasi-operatic song to a song that was more jazz, so more Afro-American orientated.

The contours of form and the distribution of dress rules can vary considerably from one clothing genre to another, as the move from the Suit to Black tie will illustrate. One change is the greater control over what it is regarded as being 'properly' dressed. This means that with Black tie the rules governing what should be worn are strictly enforced, both subjectively (no risks are taken when dressing) and objectively at the door. The compression of formal elements brings, in the case of Black tie, the outfit closer to ideal completion. The following quote signals what was earlier referred to as a differential increase in the formal integration of the Suit and Black tie: All men, although from different ranks of society, at least visually and superficially are united by convention. Increases in formal compression draw dress towards a greater degree of uniformity. Always black and white' for Black tie, but for the Suit 'we prefer white but other pale shades are acceptable. The desire to create an homogenous presence takes Black tie wearers to the very limits of civilian conformity. We put on shoes automatically, but thought enters the moment we have to decide what sort of shoes to select for a particular outfit. Greater control of an outfit's content decreases the incidence of permitted variability, with the result that dress starts to exhibit a high degree of uniformity.

The 'fit' between occasion and dress differs considerably between the Suit and Black tie. While the suit is acceptable in a variety of situations, with perhaps the most important being work, Black tie is appropriate only for a restricted range of events, all of which fall outside of work. These occasions are usually of an elevated nature, and one might say that Black tie is a sartorial response to these special events; it is the look men adopt for these singular occasions.

In the tradition of Western aesthetics, form and formal carry an idea of unity, a unity that will fluctuate according to differing degrees of integration achieved by the various elements of the arrangement. The sorts of dress under examination here express a very high degree of formal integration, the consequence of which is that both the Suit and Black tie approach completion — a state to which little can be added and little can be taken away without violating the principles governing each outfit. This high level of integration means that they present themselves as completed entities, rather than as a collection of singular garments. A high degree of formal (style) integration has customarily been favoured within the Western aesthetic tradition, which may explain why the Suit and Black tie are regarded as aesthetically superior to more informal styles of male dress.

The Look of Formality

The aesthetic dimension of the Suit and Black tie has been described earlier as a 'visual analogue' of the regulatory principles of formal dress. A number of points need to be made with regards to the idea of a visual analogue and the role it plays in creating a look of formality. An analogous relationship means the look of formality rarely contains arbitrary elements that are formal simply because they have been so named by convention; but nor is there a direct relationship between regulatory formality and the look of an outfit. There are no elements with inherent formal qualities that would provide a simple empirical matching. What one is looking for are corresponding sets of relationships rather than arbitrary or unmediated physical properties. Aesthetic formality is a complex mix of physical 'stuff' and culturally determined units that are subsequently re-formed into embodiments of the principles of formal dress. For example, the colour black in Black tie is culturally determined, and if we place the black of Black tie in a wider context its 'principled' qualities start to appear. The move from the Suit to Black tie involved a greater degree of formal integration in which the ensemble was simplified, made more uniform and subject to little or no variation. If black is placed in this context it can be seen to correspond to some of the main aspects of the move from A to B. It becomes is a kind of summary, an abstraction, of all the colour variation in the Suit. Its compulsory presence in Black tie indicates its role in integrating the outfit and it makes possible uniformity with other wearers of Black tie. This will entail finding aesthetic analogues for the following principles of regulatory formality: totality, integration, completion and uniformity.

Formal and formality have always been important parts of the European discourse on aesthetics that emerged during the Renaissance. Within this tradition, they were at their most intense in places and events overtly shaped and arranged by a strong organisational principle. Several empirical consequences flowed from this view of the formal. For instance, formal gardens were, and are, places where rules of geometry and perspective override —even contradict — those of the natural order. Formality orders and shapes the garden according to the 'rules of reason'. It is a controlling strategy bent on eliminating all 'events' outside of the straight lines and right angles of the formal. This suggests that within the European tradition, the designation of something as 'formal' invokes certain aesthetic principles and therefore certain empirical consequences. Formality implies an element of control, something also at work in formal dress. The 'shaping' that results in male formal wear is one in which distinct lines and subtly ordered materials transform the physical body into the tailored contours vital to the look of both the Suit and Black tie.

Formal objects (and events) allow little, or no, ancillary occurrences beyond the limits set by the regulatory script. Male formal wear prefers outfits where, other than for the clarity of the basic form, there is little or no elaboration. 'Ancillary events' in the form of ornaments or decoration are foregone in favour of clarity of form. The permitted degree of variation is carefully controlled so that there are no great 'swings' in the appearance of any element. For example, colour is kept within a very narrow range of muted shades in the Suit, while in Black tie it is, as we have seen, black and more black. In both, colour has an all-embracing reach rather than a localised appearance. This total spread, such a prominent characteristic of the rules governing the formal composition the Suit and Black tie, finds a corresponding structure in the aesthetic make-up of formal wear. Their very names — Suit and Dinner suit — indicate that they are integrated entities rather than collections of singular garments. All garments comprising these ensembles must be seen in terms of their place within a single, overriding form.

The consequence of this 'total' regulatory regime is a unified aesthetics of integration, rather than multifarious fragments tied to single, isolated garments. This high degree of integration means that, with the Suit for instance, there are no internal edges within the outfit. Each one of its elements — other than those directly of 'suiting', the tie, shirt and shoes — is a legitimate part of the whole and subject to the integration that binds the whole. For instance, the transition from waistcoat to shirt is a move from like to like, rather than from like to unlike, as is the case from jacket to scarf. Dress integration is manifest in the rule that every part of the suit — trousers, jacket and waistcoat — must be made from the same fabric, an imperative than demonstrates integration far better than any other.

Accompanying the aesthetic of totality is an aesthetic of completion, by which is meant the addition of parts results in the creation of a 'completed' sartorial ensemble. A consequence of completion is that little or nothing may be added or removed without the completed status of the outfit being jeopardised. The removal of a single element, say the jacket from a suit, produces a condition of incompletion. Thresholds of completion vary between clothing genres. Black tie is an outfit where completion is both expected and enforced more strictly than is the case with the Suit.

When all elements of the ensemble are present the outfit closes shut. Any substantial additions, such as brightly coloured socks, excessive jewellery and gaudy waistcoats, disrupt integration and disturb the outfit's look of formality. When worn in a 'proper' and 'complete' manner, the outfit has no gaps or openings. Gaps can refer to material features such as undoing the top button of one's shirt and loosening one's tie, or a conceptual gap, such as not wearing a hat at a time when men went about hatted. The incompleteness of being without a hat was such that it could cause a corresponding disturbance in those who witnessed its absence; it was something others felt as they tried to fill the gap. Completeness means that no areas — apart from the permissible randomness of the breast pocket handkerchief — are left unattended, wild or untamed; all are 'groomed' and domesticated in one way or another. Male formal wear is complete and, when fully present, lacks nothing; neither does it require supplements to make it whole.

The final aesthetic principle governing the appearance of male formalwear is uniformity of dress that is the requirement that those dressing in formal must wear almost the same set of garments. A clear illustration of this principle is the requirement that all the male members of a symphony orchestra be dressed in identical black tie outfits. What concerns the uniformity of formal wear is not the ways in which the individual elements of this dress are put together but rather the sorts of configurations and patterns of occurrence that emerge when they are being worn. Care needs to be exercised as to how one describes this 'congregation' of formal units. Uniformity, similarity and conformity all capture some aspects of the sameness exhibited by this type dress. But, to label this quality, for instance, as simply uniformity - with the suggestion that it is a species of uniform of some kind - is to misinterpret the black tie ensemble as being a sort of military-style uniform. But male formal wear differs from this type of outfit. They are not a set of clothes whose wearing is compulsory in quite the same sort of way that a military uniform is. Whilst they are required for specified 'events', it is not a form of dress whose wearing is enforceable through harsh punishments. Male formal wear is certainly collective in nature- it consists of a dress code that requires adherence- but it differs from, say a military uniform, by being a form of dress that is worn in a voluntary manner. It is a form of dress that is backed by a collective agreement that it is appropriate for a particular event or situation. It is the content of this 'agreement' that is at the basis upon which uniformity of dress rests. Male formal dress has elements of uniformity but it is not a uniform. This means that a group of men attending a black tie event is not the same as a row of uniformed soldiers.

Formality cannot exist without some degree of uniformity, and sameness is the result of some degree of shared rules of dress. Faced with a total variability of dress — such as we will see at work in casual clothing — formality cannot exist. A mythical exception to this is the picture of the forlorn 'District Commissioners of the British Empire ' 'dressing for dinner' despite being hundreds of miles from 'civilisation'. What gives this picture its poignancy is the absence of any co-dressers. The pattern of black tie dressing rests with the nature of the situations and events in which the wearers are participating. Formal dress is not something that is appropriate for any event or situation. Uniformity of dressing occurs when there is a participation in 'elevated' events that is events that are clearly differentiated from the mundane flow of daily life. The movement from wearing a suit to wearing black tie is directly related to the degree of elevation of the event in question. What is it about the situations and events that elicit the wearing of formal attire? What is the quality that they possess that makes formal dress an appropriate requirement? Dress confers being which, in this case, means being 'elevated' and participating in a common ritual, at the centre of which lies the formal attire of the participants. The 'point' of dress uniformity is to make manifest, and at the same time be part of, the joint being of the wearers. To dress in male formal wear is not just to signal similarity and sameness to others. (Of course, it does do this.) But to wear these clothes is to be placed in that condition

Extramural Forming

Having reached the border of this discussion of male formal dress, the simplest thing to do would be to draw this section to a close with a few concluding remarks. But the 'forming' impulse, that compression of rule and material so characteristic of the move from Suit to Black tie, is active in male dress types in regions other than those inhabited by conventional clothing. Common threads are at work in the most unlikely of bedfellows.

These extramural formings are of two sorts: those manifest in the life of a collective of some kind, and those in the actions of an individual. With regards to the former, perhaps the clearest example of forming power lies with the military. The foundation upon which all of its daily routines rest is the creation of a mass of undifferentiated units dressed in identical uniform. This creation of uniformity is brought about by the full mobilisation of a quality that has been flickering in the margins throughout this discussion of formal attire — semi-compulsory uniformity. This mass of identical units moves about in the geometric patterns common to military ceremonies, ceremonies that are composed of precision, order, detail and design.

The forming I wish to discuss in some detail, though, is the individual forming practised by dandies. Traditionally, the dandy occupied an ambiguous position in relation to conventional male dress. He was contemptuous of 'acceptable' forms of bourgeois male dress, while at the same time practising a meticulous form of dressing, the aim of which was to improve upon the very clothes he professed to dislike. Dandies were isolated individuals, both sartorially and philosophically, who used dress and dressing as a means of articulating a philosophy of perfection, and with it a critique of everything that fell short of this standard in society at large. It was in the operations of taste that dandies acted out their criticisms by deed. The idea that the dandy was an exuberant and eccentric dresser has, thankfully, been put to rest. Above all, what distinguished the dandy was not the novelty of the garments he wore (although this did happen on occasion) but the increased pressure he brought to bear in applying the rules governing the conventional forms of male dress. What is distinctive about the dandy is that the stringent application of dress rules was self-administered; it was a voluntary continuation of the formal compression we saw operating earlier. The 'improvements' undertaken by the dandy almost always involved a 'tightening' of an element of dress rather than a 'loosening', or by its wholesale replacement with a novel garment. Shared rules and conventions were replaced by self-administered standards. There was an acceptance of the broad framework of male formal dress, but there also a desire to bring it closer to perfection or to what I have called total completion. The dandy saw his task as one in which he constantly scrutinised his dress for elements in need of completion. This explains why the dandy was so concerned with the details of his dress. Attention to detail is the one area where there was space for his perfecting urge to do its work.

As always when discussing dandies, an anecdote about Beau Brummell is particularly instructive. One morning a visitor called on Brummell, whom he found still dressing at a late hour. The visitor couldn't help noticing a pile of neck cloths on the floor. When he asked what was going on, Brummell's manservant replied: 'Those are failures sir'. Brummell's search for the strategic detail, in this case the neckcloth, is followed and it draws him towards perfection. Something so elevated as the search for perfection is bound to have its failures. Brummell's acceptance of the neckcloth and his subsequent search for its perfection is in sharp contrast to its rejection by Wilkes and his circle.

This search for perfection through formal completion often does not remain within the limits of the dressed body. It is as if the dressed body is able to set up a 'sphere of influence' into which objects and, in some cases, whole locations are drawn. The wish is to re-form the world and its objects into an aesthetically coherent and highly integrated environment. This 'completion' often takes the form of total saturation of a 'world' by a single style. What distinguishes the dandies' forming is the ever-broadening scope of its perfecting designs, a scope that must eventually falter and dissipate in the face of a world forever in a state of disrepair.

This trajectory can be seen in the behaviour and habits of the renowned American cancer surgeon W.S. Halsted (1852–1922). Halsted was a truly bizarre character who exhibited many dandyish traits, in particular the precision he exercised in purchasing his clothes and the lengths he went to maintaining them in a presentable condition:

In Baltimore he was always extraordinarily careful of his attire. Every detail was guarded — every suit of clothes, and he had dozens of them, was made by the best tailor in London. His shoes he had made in Paris, for some strange reason — and there he insisted on selecting the particular place in a skin from which he would have the leather cut. When six pairs of shoes arrived in Baltimore he examined them closely and sometimes recognized a failure on the part of the shoemaker to adhere strictly to his orders so far as the choice of leather was concerned. Such a pair of shoes was cast aside and never worn. Shirts he had made at Charvet's in great numbers from carefully chosen material, and these were for years sent to Paris to be laundered. (10)

His desire for perfection didn't stop with dress. It flowed into his domestic environment. Only he was allowed to arrange the dinner table when there were guests; his wife was forbidden to have anything to do with organising the meal. The tablecloth was always closely scrutinised for creases, and if any were found it had to be ironed on the table. Every detail of the meal was subject to Halsted's punishing standards. In the end his wife put a stop to this behaviour so as to spare him the physical exhaustion that set in after the occasion was over. Eventually, as Halsted's predicament illustrates, the forming urge will exhaust itself and weaken as it comes up against just too much 'world' presenting itself for perfection.

Varieties of the Informal

The simplest and most direct approach to formal and informal dress is through form. Formal dress covers those sorts of attire in possession of form, while informal dress covers those where form is thought to be either absent or greatly reduced. No matter what kinds of informal clothing are being discussed, the rules, conventions and aesthetics of formal wear constitute a benchmark against which the various kinds of informal are measured. This is because the *principles* that make up male formal wear are logically prior to the principles that make up the informal. The informal lacks the aesthetic skeleton provided by form, as well as a regulated agreement as to what an 'appropriate' style of wearing might be. But if we ask what the informal consists of, we will find that not only does the simple picture of presence and absence of form need modification, but also the very category of the informal amounts to a great deal more than a story of absence.

Informal dress can be separated into two types: 'designated' informal, a type of clothing often referred to as 'casual', and the 'non-formal'. Casual clothing consists of garments that are specifically designed to be informal, while the non-formal includes conditions of dress that result either from the actions of the wearer or from the circumstances in which wearers find themselves. The non-formal is, then, generally to do with the manner in which the clothes are being worn rather than with the presence of specific garments.

Just as the move from Suit to Black tie involved ever-increasing measures of form, informal dress can be characterised by its opposite. There is a diminution, sometimes gradual, sometimes abrupt, of form. Each instance of informality assumed by male dress might be thought of as a *departure*, or falling away, from an ideal stemming from the principles of formal attire. (Non-adherence to the rules of the formal can mean a greater degree of variability is permitted at any point in one's dress, but it does not mean a free-for-all. Some types of informality are shared and followed — particularly casual wear — not as regulated, codified elements, but rather as a result of the cohesive force of fashion.) The differentiation of one's dress from the formal ideal can be the result of intention, as with wearing casual wear, or negligence, simple forgetfulness, or it may arise from a set of circumstances that make adherence to the ideal impossible. A common feature of informal male dress is a decrease of integration among the various garments that comprise an outfit. Dress moves away from obeying the imperative of completion so central to formal wear, and instead leans towards being permanently 'unfinished'. The informal, in both its designated and non-formal modes, is characterised by decreased compression of the garments comprising an outfit where clothes are joined into an 'appropriate' series.

The reception of this 'unfinished' or open-ended condition is not always favourable. Formal dress can receive terms of approval such as 'neat', 'smart', 'tidy', 'elegant' and 'well dressed'. These adjectives acknowledge the satisfactory completion of dressing or they may refer to the minor actions of 'tidying up' required to achieve complete dressing. Informal dressing can often attract derogatory adjectives such as 'shabby', 'untidy', 'scruffy', 'unkempt', 'unseemly' and 'inappropriate', and, of course, 'dirty'. These disparaging adjectives either draw attention to an absence of some kind — for instance, trainers instead of 'proper' shoes — or the presence of something that should not be there, such as a poorly ironed shirt. Shabby conditions, if we may call them that, come about either because the wearer has not paid enough attention to grooming or because he is wearing an inappropriate set of garments. Dress that attracts derogatory adjectives lacks the qualities of the formal ideal against which they are being measured. 'Elegant' is not a word often applied to informal types of dress.

What I propose to do in the remainder of this section is trace some of the pathways taken by the designated informal (casual wear) and the non-formal. Examining the distance that lies between them and the ideal against which they are measured and judged will do this. Unlike male formal dress, where the central feature is one of an increasing integration of dress, the examples of the informal examined here follow their own particular disintegrative pathways. I should make it clear that this is not a comprehensive examination of the full range of informalities. There are others, each of which has its own specific 'distance' from the formal.

Elementary

In front of me are two photographs of my father and his friend taken a short time after one another. It is the early 1950s in the south of England. The day is hot and the two men have adjusted their dress to better cope with the heat. In the first photograph my father is wearing a semi-formal outfit of a sports jacket and a pair of trousers known as flannels, or slacks. He has unbuttoned his jacket and removed his tie. He is wearing his shirt collar folded outside his jacket collar — the style so carefully avoided by the television presenters. In the second photograph the men's adjustments have progressed even further. Their jackets have been removed and they have draped them over their shoulders. The final adjustment my father has made has been to roll up his shirtsleeves.

What is taking place in the photographs is a journey from the semi-formal outfit of sports jacket and flannels to a set of informal responses to the hot weather. It would be wrong to be too dismissive of any functional explanation for these adjustments; there is no doubt the adjustments enabled the wearer to better cope with the hot weather. But more is happening here than simply temperature control. The adjustments all worked on certain features of formal dress and it is these adjustments, and the absence of a number of formal dress features, that propel the wearer into the informal. The two men are engaged in a series of functional actions, but they are also deploying a set of informal adjustments to their dress that speaks of the greater freedom than even these elementary gestures can bring about. The elementary informal emerges from within the conventional formality of male dress.

Above and beyond a cooling function, each adjustment performed by the two men symbolically enacts the liberation of the informal from the 'restrictions' of formal dress. The informal is not without structure. Opening the shirt down to the waist would be frowned upon. Wearing the jacket open is a breach in the 'all-over' covering so fundamental to the suit. To take off the jacket is an adjustment that removes the wearer from the formal sphere altogether and ushers in a radical reordering of the rules governing the upper part of the body. An important part of the aesthetic of the suit is that it keeps the scaffolding of dress hidden; the removal of the jacket reveals the confluence of belt, trousers, braces and shirt in a brutal display of functional scaffolding. Most adjustments common to the elementary informal occupy an ambiguous position somewhere between the formal and informal. The wearer's articulation of the informal is rudimentary, having only a partial understanding of what is involved in the adjustments to dress. They do not know that they are informal.

If we return to the first photograph, the most obvious adjustment my father makes to his dress is the collar — now tieless — worn outside the jacket collar. I know of no viable functional explanation for wearing one's collar in this way. It is a fashion drifting somewhere between the two orders of dress, a gesture of pure style that belongs to neither. Exactly what is taking place with this 'warm weather' fashion and where precisely its informality lies is not easy to determine. A comparison with the tieless fashion of the television presenters discussed earlier may throw some light on the issue. In the case of the male presenters, the shirt collar never appears above the jacket, and the only evidence of informality is the absence of the tie and the consequences this has for the neck region. No presenter ever appears wearing the shirt collar in the manner my father does, and there is little doubt that such a style would be regarded as unacceptable. My sense of why this style is avoided is that it would draw the wearer near to styles of masculinity regarded as unfashionable or unsavoury. The fact that television presenters work in climate-controlled environments makes any functional explanation for the removal of the tie invalid. In the case of my father's response to the heat, it is the removal of the tie not the placement of the collar that serves to cool the body. The position taken up by the collar might be a general sign of summer and all that this implies: heat, leisure, relaxation, and freedom. It may be an aesthetic response to the removal of the tie, the collar no longer supporting or supported by the tie. With this formal task gone, the collar is able to travel to places not determined by formal dress. While it may be pure style, the migration of the collar into the open is an indication that new types of dress are being created and this new territory belongs to informal dress, not to formal.

In the second photograph, my father and his friend have completed the adjustments to their dress with the still-common practice of rolling up one's shirtsleeves. Once again we have the manipulation of one's dress with a dual gesture of comfort and freedom. The male body, via informal adjustments, starts to emerge from beneath its formal covering and presents a sharp contrast to the enveloped body so skilfully engineered by the suit. Rolling up one's shirtsleeves is a presentiment of what was to arrive with casual wear — garments with built-in rolled up sleeves. The elementary informal looks to the rules and aesthetics of formal dress, and through 'adjusting' certain of these features we can observe the emergence of the informal. But when the nature of these intentional and self-administered adjustments are examined — rolling up of one's shirtsleeves for instance — the suggestion of casual wear is not far away. Because, in the photographs, the informal was being played out on clothes of a formal nature, the drive towards the casual is buried in the moves of the elementary informal. The removal of the jacket, the rolling up of the shirtsleeves and the absence of a tie were about claiming a degree of freedom — the most important selling point of casual wear.

At this point in his life my father possessed no casual wear. It did not exist for men of his class at that time. He had no specialised leisure clothing, so the creation of informality rested upon a set of sanctioned adjustments to his already existing dress. This meant that the only avenue available was via the sorts of adjustments visible in the photographs. This kind of informality is elementary because it sets about creating informality from the formal materials it has at hand.

Casual

Casual: accidental; unexpected; temporary; unceremonious; relaxed; associated with leisure
The New Shorter Oxford Dictionary

Casual, in short, is everything male formal attire attempts to repress and avoid. It is clear from this abbreviated dictionary entry that casual wear belongs to a very different world to that of formal dress. It is an order of clothing in which chance and the accidental can happen and where the passage of time means a constant rearrangement of what is worn and the manner of it's wearing. This is in sharp contrast to formal attire, where the golden rule is constancy of dress. Casual wear, following a pattern examined earlier, defines itself through affirmation and negation. At its most basic is a declaration that casual is not formal, but this assertion opens it to a number of positive qualities such as 'relaxed', 'leisure', 'temporary' and 'comfort'. Casual wear has always been sited in a number of imaginary locations (purveyed by the advertising industry) and accompanied by a set of somatic dispositions that are radically different to those of formal wear. If the Suit is associated with work and Black tie with elevated social occasions then casual wear is found in a number of imaginary scenarios where a wearer is released from strict dress regulation into a realm of relaxed informality. It is this sartorial liberation that sits at the centre of casual wear and enables the wearer to participate in a variety of leisure-inflected states and activities. (11) The formal, on the other hand, keeps the wearer to a single, or very limited range, of being. Being formal.

Any understanding of casual wear for males needs to take into consideration the place, date and social class of the wearer. In each country, the route taken by the emergence and spread of casual wear could differ considerably. In the country I am most familiar with, the United Kingdom, small quantities of casual clothing began to be imported from the mid–1950s onwards. It originated in America and Italy, and to begin with was the chosen dress of small urban groups. (12) The journey from highly restricted distribution to domination of male dress unfolded over the next two decades, and such has been its penetration of the male wardrobe that it is almost impossible to imagine either a place or a time where casual dress were absent and unavailable to the majority of the male population. The trends driving this expansion in men's casual attire were many and various. Certainly greater disposable income, more leisure time, especially the increase in overseas holidays, all played a part. In fact, a case could be made for the rise in the popularity of casual wear being a sartorial response to the new climates encountered during Mediterranean holidays. Other trends fuelling its spread were the arrival of much cheaper clothing, and hence the expansion of the male wardrobe, and, one suspects, men's greater attention to their appearance.

It is not by chance that many styles of casual wear had their origins in the types of dress associated with upper-class sports. As well as the social cachet that attached to these garments, more importantly they provided a blueprint for clothing designed solely for leisure. Of course, these clothes of the elite have drifted away from their original context — for instance, the garments are no longer simply worn for the duration of the game. Once they become items of casual wear they are worn according to the rhythms familiar to other items of clothing. A good example of this drift is the Lacoste shirt. It was designed in 1933 to be worn on the tennis court to provide the player with a degree of comfort in the face of heat and perspiration. By the early 1960s, along with the Fred Perry tennis shirt, it had become a compulsory Mod accessory in London and other British cities. Not long after this restricted sub-cultural location was established, the male population at large took up the shirt. As well as the emergence of specialised casual clothing, a later appropriation occurred of clothing initially designed for intense athletic activities — such as tracksuits and trainers — and this transformed into casual wear. My first encounter with this use of sports wear in casual fashion was on a Spanish campsite in 1968. The male members of a nearby French family were dressed in *Le Coq Sportif* athletic garments. There was never any sign that physical activity was about to take place.

As we saw earlier, the very name 'casual' conjures up a number of qualities quite distinct from those of formal wear. Indeed, casual gains it's meaning from being in clear opposition to the formal. Perhaps the most significant difference between the two orders is the absence, in casual wear, of a highly codified set of rules and conventions governing how one should dress. This does not mean the various states assumed by informality of dress are arbitrary; casual dressing is not a free for all. It means the individual's personal choice is the basis of what is worn, rather than sartorial legislation. The rules and aesthetics of dress totality, which are so central to male formal dress, are not present with casual wear. Despite the efforts of the fashion industry, there is no set of 'overall' rules that defines the form taken by an outfit. Apart from the minimal requirement that one should be dressed, there are no aesthetic standards legislating how an individual will dress overall. Because of this freedom, emphasis is placed to a much greater extent upon the selection of individual garments rather than the dictates of coherent wholes. This means that the degree of integration in casual wear is considerably less than in formal wear. There are no regulations governing what item of clothing goes where; one garment has no idea what will move in next to it.

Casual clothing is not just a collection of 'informal' garments. It carries an invitation to wear the garments in an informal manner. Part of the garments' promise lay in the way they encouraged their purchaser to adopt a whole set of somatic postures and physical dispositions. It is rare, for instance, to see someone in Black tie performing any form of strenuous physical exercise, unless it is part of a heavily ironical advertisement. Purchasing casual clothing means one is also purchasing abstract qualities such as 'freedom', 'leisure' and 'relaxation'. The suit, while an excellent outfit for the demands of the urban public sphere, simply does not fit with the forms of activity, even the ways of being, that are an integral part of casual dress.

Scruffy

In July 2012, a story titled 'Last Train to Scruffsville' appeared in the *Sydney Morning Herald*. It reported that the New South Wales' Minister of Transport had issued a warning to all uniformed staff of the state's rail system (known as Railcorp) that they were 'to comply with grooming standards' or face punishment. A list of 'grooming violations' was set out so that each employee would know where and when they were breaking the grooming code. These violations were:

> Sunglasses pushed up onto one's forehead
> Long sleeves rolled up
> Wearing summer blouses in winter
> Wearing shirts untucked
> Wearing pullovers around the waist
> Facial hair not 'neatly trimmed'
> Hats and caps not worn at a 'proper angle'

Management would be responsible for enforcing grooming regulations, and any employee caught breaching the rules could be sent home for the rest of the day. The rationale for the introduction of this dress code was a belief that a smart workforce was an efficient workforce, or, more likely, the look of a smart workforce would give the impression of a well-run, efficient organisation. Of course, the corollary of this is the assumption that 'scruffy' employees are inefficient workers.

Adjectives such as 'scruffy', 'untidy' and 'unkempt' indicate some form of departure has taken place from the ideal manner of wearing, in this case, the uniform of Railcorp. The uniform, or an equivalent set of sponsored clothes, becomes a sartorial ideal against which departures are measured and, most importantly, judged. This index of derogatory informality is primarily concerned with how clothes are worn rather than with the presence of specific garments. The derogatory core in each adjective comes from its referral to either the presence of something that should be absent — for example, facial stubble — or to the absence of something that should be present — for example, a necktie.

Scruffy informal can be an intentional or habitual modification of one's clothing in the direction of lesser formality; for example, rolling up one's shirtsleeves or wearing one's shirt untucked from one's trousers. The aim of these voluntary and intentional modifications is to propel the wearer farther into a state of informality. They may be undertaken to increase the wearer's physical comfort, but they can also be enacted to open up a space between the wearer and the institution of which they are a part. A too fastidious adherence to official dress code may indicate an overly close identification with the employer. This means little or no room is left for wearers to insert their individuality into the daily round. In this instance, scruffy informality can be an expression of personal identity. (Slovenly defiance, perhaps.) Departures from the endorsed form of dress may come about through reluctance to conform, from indifference or simply through forgetfulness. For instance, rolling up one's shirtsleeves may result from any one of these reasons. One may become scruffy — only washing clothes intermittently or not ironing — through forgetfulness, indifference or deliberate omission.

Unlike other kinds of the informal, scruffy is a form of judgment. So some kind of rule must be present for evaluation to take place. To call someone scruffy implies that they are failing to conform to some 'non-scruffy' state. The condition can be rectified if the 'scruff' performs some work to eradicate their sartorial deficiencies to align their condition with the endorsed ideal. Scruffy informal appears when the ideal (regularised) form of wearing is compared with the actual manner of wearing to ascertain how far the latter has drifted from the former. A judgment of 'scruffy' comes from the disparity between what is and what should be. In the case of Railcorp, punishment may be applied according to the distance between the two.

Forlorn

Forlorn: abandoned; forsaken; ruined; hopeless
The Concise Oxford Thesaurus

Unlike the sorts of informal dress looked at so far, with forlorn dress there is no hope or possibility that the divide between what 'should be' and what 'is' will ever be brought back into alignment. Likewise, its wearers have no hope of escaping the state of abandonment in which they find themselves. What they are wearing will never be restored to how it was before catastrophe struck.

On 15 February 1942, the commander of the defeated British forces in Singapore, Lieutenant General Arthur Percival, set off to negotiate a surrender with the Japanese military command. For several days Percival and his staff had been kept in isolation. Eventually, they were made to walk past lines of Empire and Japanese troops carrying a flag of truce on their way to sign the official documents of defeat. It is their appearance during this 'surrender walk' (tellingly they did not march) that speaks most eloquently of their hopeless situation. During their isolation they had been deprived of servants, especially servants whose job it was to maintain their uniforms by washing and ironing, and by the frequent use of starch. At the end of its isolation, the British high command appeared far beyond inconsequential shabbiness. Sweat stains, dirty markings and extensive creasing all added to an air of abdication. Degradation of one's dress was a powerful supplement to the degrading situation that Percival and his men found themselves in. Their forlorn appearance was in contrast to that of the Japanese soldiers, who were turned out in neat, clean uniforms and looked every inch the victors.

Forlorn informality, and the poignancy that accompanies it, comes out of the tragic destruction of what was once an impressive and coherent style of dress — in the case outlined above, military uniform. Although all forlorn dress exhibits a gulf between what was and what is, it is still possible to reconstruct its original form using the ruined remains currently worn. It is this disintegration, along with the ability to discern where it has fallen from, that is the source of the poignancy of forlorn dress. Its tragedy lies in the impossibility of restoring it to its original state. In the case of the British in Singapore, what had previously been the dress of status and power (of the Empire) had collapsed into emblems of defeat and hopelessness. Forlorn dress differs from other types of the informal because of the magnitude of the effect it has on the standing of the 'perfect' form of dress and the emotional feelings that accompany its descent into ruination. These strong emotions are absent from the other forms of informal dress, where departures from dress codes were occasionally subject to sanctions, but did not involve the complete collapse of a dress regime, as happened with the fall of Singapore. What took place there was not a voluntary decline. The departures from the ideal were stages in a process of degradation, a much more serious consequence than a simple violation of a local dress code. Unlike scruffy informal — the case with Railcorp — forlorn dress cannot be rectified by simply pulling its wearer into line and then sending them home for the rest of the day.

There could be no better indication of the collapse of Imperial power than the state of the uniforms of the British high command. The clothing of surrender speaks of abandonment; servants will no longer come to the rescue and begin to wash, iron and starch, tasks essential for the 'proper' appearance of uniforms. As British power evaporated, sweat stains appeared and spread. As command vanished, the cut of the tropical shorts disappeared into a forest of creases.

In many ways the surrender of Singapore, where there is degradation of a whole outfit, is unusual. The forlorn is more likely to come in a fragmentary and fleeting form, as can be seen towards the end of Luchino Visconti's adaptation of Thomas Mann's novella, *Death in Venice* (1971).

The artist Aschenbach has what, in modern parlance, is called a makeover. His hair and moustache are dyed and his face is 'adjusted' with rouge and powder and lipstick. Why he submits to this artifice remains ambiguous. Either he wants to make himself attractive to the young boy, Tadeusz, who has come to occupy the whole of his imagination, or, and I think this is more likely, he is trying to acquire for himself the beauty that he sees in the young boy. Before long his 'improvements' unravel, the most unsettling of which is the trail of hair dye that runs down his cheek and threatens to destroy the integrity of his beautiful white suit. It is at that moment that the forlorn swings open. The marks from the hair dye unlock the grotesque effects produced by his attempt to become beautiful. The forlorn resides in this disintegration of Aschenbach's vision of absolute beauty and in the collapse of sartorial perfection echoed in the marks on this cheek and shirt collar. Nothing and no one can enter Aschenbach's transcendent vision of beauty. He is impervious to the grotesque effect that his search for the beautiful has had on his face and which promises to ruin the purity of his suit. It is not long before we learn he is dying, and the grotesque 'adjustments to his face produced by dyes, powders and rouge will no longer be of any consequence. Only death will redeem his forlorn state.

Beyond Informality

In her book *A Place of Greater Safety* Hilary Mantel describes the sorts of dress that lie beyond those we have described as informal. I hesitate here, unsure that 'worn' and 'dress' in this context are the correct way to describe the relationship between the body and the materials it is in contact with:

He moved to a chair, unable to drag his eyes from the scrap of humanity that was the Citizeness Albertine. Her garments were funereal layers, an array of wraps and shawls, belonging to no style or fashion that had ever existed.(13)

Mantel alights on two features of the coverings found in the territory beyond formality. First, the individual is 'clothed' in layers and wraps rather than with fitted garments. Second, the outfit owes no allegiance any style or fashion. It is indebted purely to itself.

All those types of dress I have called informal contain some kind of unravelling of the rules and aesthetic principles associated with formal attire. Even in the case of forlorn dress, the poignancy came from a contrast between what was and what is; we are confronted with a ruined coherence. But is it possible for sartorial integration to be completely absent, and if it is then does dress itself disappear? It is just such a condition that Mantel describes in the quotation above. The kinds of 'clothing' and styles of 'wearing' adopted by the poor and homeless in countries with colder climates no longer defers to an ideal. There is, as Mantel says, no style or fashion and therefore no ideal dress referent to govern what is being worn. There is no degradation *from* anything. What we have is not about loss, as we saw in forlorn dress, but more about not having. The consequence is that there is no interest in establishing any level of coherence among the garments and materials being 'worn'. There is rawness in the way that the coverings and the wearer intersect. The ensemble has no polish, no integration. It lies outside of all these things. The body disappears into the collection of materials and garments and reappears in a variety of peculiar, non-clothed shapes, in the sense of not wearing clothes. Styles, fashions etcetera are stripped of their context and are made to rest alongside one another in bizarre contiguity. The poor and the homeless will wear what is given or found, not what fits with one's taste or with rules and conventions of particular outfits. This sartorial condition can, like forlorn dress, evoke strong emotions on the part of those who encounter it. Pity certainly is a component, a reaction to the absence of integration, even shape itself, in what is being worn. Wearing clothing that is completely devoid of integration and devoted solely to keeping the body warm often presents the wearer in a set of grotesque shapes. What we see are human beings wearing clothing as a defence against the weather, and to do this they pile of on what they can find. We, having the benefit of shelter, can wear clothing that plays around with acceptable body shapes. We are 'normal' because we have clothing built into the heating systems of our homes and places of work. They are a reminder of the distortions necessary to stay alive without shelter. To survive often means those qualities of dress such as integration, ideal, form, fashion and code are absent.

In this deliberately restricted exercise that was intentionally formalist, it was never intended to be a total examination of formality and informality. My aim has been to test the validity of Tseelon's assertion that formality/ formal and informality/informal are exhausted categories capable only of 'stereotypical thinking', bereft of any purchase on empirical reality. My opinion, of course, is that this is not the case, but it is with the reader, not the author, who must exercise their judgment on this question.

Notes and References

(1) Efra Tseelon, 'Is Identity a Useful Tool?' in *Critical Studies in Fashion and Beauty*, vol. 1, no. 2, Leeds, 2010, p. 156.

(2) Alan Flusser, *Dressing the Man: Mastering the Art of Permanent Fashion*, HarperCollins, New York, 2001.

(3) B. Brumett, *The Rhetoric of Machine Aesthetics*, Greenwood Publishing Group, 1999, pp. 100–101.
Elizabeth Diller and Ricardo Scofidio, *Bad Press: Dissident Ironing*, 1993–98; www.youtube.com/watch?v=Ozz4Kpqrh9M, an amusing performance piece by two North American architects.

(4) See Thorstein Veblen, *The Theory of the Leisure Class*, (1994), New York, Penguin and Georg Simmel, 'The Philosophy of Fashion', in *Simmel on Culture*, Frisby and Featherstone, 1997, Sage London.

(5) Elizabeth Wilson, *Adorned in Dreams*, Virago, London, 1985; and B*ohemians: The Glamorous Outcasts*, Tauris Peke, London, 2000.

(6) Tom Wolfe, *Kandy-Kolored Tangerine-Flake Streamline Baby*, Farrar, Strauss & Giroux, New York, 1965, p. 8.

(7) Richard Sennett, *The Fall of Public Man*, Cambridge University Press, 1977.

(8) Don De Lillo, *White Noise*, Picador, London, 2011, p. 247.

(9) Robin Dutt, 'Men's Formal Wear', in Valerie Steele (ed.), *The Berg Companion to Fashion*, Berg, Oxford, 2000, pp. 349–351.

1(0) W.G. MacCallum and W.H. Welch, *William Stewart Halsted, Surgeon*, Johns Hopkins Press, Baltimore, 1930, pp. 105–107.

(11) Clothing scholar, J.C. Flugel, made an interesting contribution to the archaeology of men's casual wear. In the 1930s, he mounted a prescient criticism of the male suit, which he characterised as drab, unhygienic and conformist. Flugel, mixing the functional with the aesthetic, urged men to reform their dress with a degree of urgency. He was of the opinion that women's dress that could provide a template for the reformers of male dress. Flugel argued that many of the qualities of women's dress, such as a greater variety of colour, wider range of materials, use of patterned materials, greater response to external circumstances, more personal choice and a greater exposure of the body could be imported with advantage into male dress. Pattern does not seem to have been taken up to a great

extent by men. The wonderful exception to this is the Hawaiian shirt. All of these qualities gradually made an appearance in male casual dress after World War II. To my knowledge, this relationship between female dress and male casual dress has remains unexplored. See J.C. Flugel, *The Psychology of Clothes*, Hogarth Press, London, 1930

(12) Nik Cohn, *Today There Are No Gentlemen*, Weidenfeld and Nicholson, London, 1971. Also Richard Weight, *Mod: A Very British Style*, Bodley Head, London, 2013.

(13) Hilary Mantel, *A Place of Greater Safety*, Fourth Estate, London, p. 820.

Chapter Six

Upstairs, Downstairs:
The Comings and Goings of Dress

Come down when you're ready dear.
Kingsley Amis; *The Old Devils*

For the inhabitants of the rich, capitalist countries of the West, the clothes we wear are part of an ever-changing stream of garments that appear on the horizon of affordability only to eventually disappear at the hands of taste. Likewise, the bodies that 'fill out' this procession of garments are forever shifting shape and so vanish with every change of clothes.

Dress, and it's coming into being, is about much more than the ebb and flow of the physical 'stuff' that make up the garments and bodies of their wearers. Dress is about how we extend ourselves beyond the mundane, of how we transform the physicality of bodies and 'stuff' into decidedly immaterial states. It is to the life cycle of dress, how it emerges and how it unravels, that is the subject of this chapter.

Dress or Covering?

Two images to begin with. The first, a photograph of a child was taken at height of the war in Chechnya in 1995. The absence of trousers — that is, what the child is *not* wearing — suggests this is a young girl, but ultimately gender remains indeterminate. Several children had been hiding in a cellar in Grozny, the capital of Chechnya, for a number of weeks and the photograph shows the exact moment they emerged from their hiding place.

Illustration 1
Grozny Child: 1995

Illustration 2
Royal Horse Guards: 1835

Illustration 2 depicts Major Everard William Bouverie of the Royal Horse Guard in full uniform in 1835. If we compare the 'coverings' of the Grozny child with the sumptuous uniform of Major Bouverie, fundamental differences are obvious in the ways in which they have chosen to cover their bodies and make them visible. In the case of the Royal Horse Guard, and despite the surfeit of decoration, the uniform and its wearer display a unified, formal whole. There is a sense in which decoration is deployed in the name of what it is decorating, becoming the public face for the whole figure. Rather than creating an embellished 'thin' surface, the decoration together with the form of the uniform establishes a degree of depth, drawing the body of the wearer into the totality of his dress. (1)

If we look at what the Grozny child wears, a number of features distinguish it from Major Bouverie and his uniform. Her 'covering' is indifferent to being seen; that is, she is not dressed in the sense of being part of a group, where bodily adjustments are organised according to a set of communally held rules. There is no 'communication' between the body and it's covering, as is the case with Bouverie and his uniform. Its surface carries no indication that the body is drawn into the organisation of the ensemble — indeed, the body seems utterly absorbed by its need for protection. Her covering is little more than a protective sheath on the point of losing what little formal coherence it ever possessed.

On the one hand, we have a uniformed figure dressed in a style of clothing that's premised on its need to display luxuriant decoration and formal clarity. In short, the uniform lives and breathes as something to be seen. On the other hand, the Grozny child's covering exhibits none of the preparation or readiness found in 'proper' dress. It is more suited to a 'blind' environment, something akin to the cellar the children were forced to hide in. The child is covered, but I'm not at all sure she is dressed.

Getting Dressed

If someone tells you to get dressed, what do you have to do to comply with this demand? And, what state are you in before getting dressed?

Dress, and its many dimensions, sits at the heart of what follows. It plays a central role in the two major themes of this chapter: the coming into being of dress and its subsequent unravelling. Dress may be thought of as referring to all those bodily adjustments — both additions and subtractions — that are the 'elementary particles' required for the condition of being dressed. There always needs to be some bodily adjustment, however small, to mark the transition into *being dressed*. But dress is not just the sum of these bodily adjustments; it also means a 'making ready', a preparation of the individual who wears these adjustments. But making ready for what? Being prepared for what occasion?

Being dressed, in the sense of made ready, means being prepared for encounters with individuals who are also dressed, preferably in a manner similar to oneself. Dress is an essential ingredient to all forms of communal life. It can mean wearing anything — a pair of pyjamas, work clothes or a dinner suit. Dressing is a continuous preparation for the next encounter; a never-ending alignment of dress to the requirements of the situation one finds oneself in. (2)

Raw Materials

At the start of his novel *Sartor Resartus*, Thomas Carlyle has the main character Dr Teufelsdrockh subject to a disturbing insight into the clothes he is wearing — and by implication the clothes worn by our species as a whole:

While I — Good heavens — have thatched myself over with dead fleeces, the bark of vegetables, the entrails of worms, the hides of oxen and seals, the felt of furred beasts: and walk abroad a moving Rag-screen, over heaped with shreds and tatters raked from the Charnel house of nature, where they would have rotted, to rot on me more slowly. (3)

What is so telling about this vision is the way in which Teufelsdrockh's imagination (or Carlyle's) is able to go back over all the stages that the *coming into being of dress* has passed through. Eventually, he encounters the raw materials out of which our clothing has emerged. The interval that inevitably lies between raw material and finished clothing was of great import to Carlyle. He regarded our fashioning of nature into a manmade 'fleece' as essential to our being. Alone in all of nature, we are the sole species to 'work' the raw materials provided by nature to bring them closer to our needs and desires. This is why dress is one of our most distinctive features. For Carlyle, dress lay somewhere between the 'Charnel house of nature' and the screams of the animals supplying raw materials and the middens where rotting garments were changed into unformed matter.

Object

Making dress, in the sense of what gets worn, is not just the application of a set of manual skills to material stuff. There is a third dimension, a non-material dimension, where potential is to be found; this 'non-material' dimension is realised when the garment is ready to be worn. As will become clear later, the ability of these dress components to embody an ideal, a form and a style is the first intimation of the propulsive power of sublimation. (4)

Dress objects are not undifferentiated pieces of inert, physical stuff. As well as embodying material and skill, they have a dimension concerned with 'completion': the potential to become what they are intended to be. They are 'open' objects that will only be 'closed' when they have completed their journey to the landing, a place that will be revealed in good time. (5)

Staircases

Just as this exploration of dress has an explicit theoretical structure, which will be discussed later, so it also has a metaphorical component in the form of two staircases. These staircases, with their rich metaphorical potential, enable the abstract, conceptual 'descriptions' to assume the form of concrete images.

Illustration 3:
Powell & Pressburger 1946
A Matter of Life and Death

Illustration 4:

Rowlandson, *The Exhibition* c.1811

The first staircase (shown in ill. 3) comes from Powell and Pressburger's 1946 film, *A Matter of Life and Death*. The second (ill. 4) titled The Exhibition and created c. 1811, is from the hand of the English artist Thomas Rowlandson. On the first staircase are Allied airmen killed in action during World War II. They travel upwards, and when they reach the top an angelic bureaucrat asks them whether they would prefer 'a frock or wings'. Although we only see the airmen carrying their wings, the implication is that their battered combat clothing will drop away, to be replaced by the transcendental garments that are *de rigueur* for their new heavenly existence. The upward movement of the staircase is matched by a comparable change in the worldly clothing worn 'down below'. As there is nothing beyond heaven, the garments they are offered at the head of their upward journey represent an end to the life-long sartorial transformations of their Earthly existence. In this sense, the frock and wings are both complete and 'stable'. To ascend the staircase is to gradually become dressed for the last time.

In Rowlandson's *The Exhibition*, (c. 1800) movement down the staircase releases a number of *undressing* forces. A quite different set of dress transformations are revealed from those of the upward staircase. Being dressed at the head of the staircase gives way to a condition in which some, if not all, the elemental principles of dress have evaporated by the time they reach the bottom. The composed and sharply dressed individuals at the head of the staircase become part of a sartorial river, where garments and flesh are jumbled together. Inevitably, this heap of individuals in a state of *deshabille* allows us to see what should not be seen and for dress to be drastically bent out of shape, its cohesion dissipated. As we descend the staircase, the coherence and adhesion of the various ensembles start to weaken. The rules governing what should be placed next to what vanish, allowing the garments to 'separate' from one another as well as from the wearer's body. The garments begin to exist independently of one another, meaning that, in a strict sense, the body is no longer *dressed*. It is the plummet Earthwards that has undone them.

So, dressed at the head of the staircase and undressed as they tumble towards the bottom.

Sublimation and Sublation

If the figure of the staircase has provided dress with a metaphorical colouring, sublimation and, to a much lesser extent, sublation provides a more conventional theoretical foundation to the discussion. (Desublimation will be discussed later.)

Aside from their presence in specialised scientific discourse, sublation and sublimation have a restricted distribution in the English language. Sublate is a term confined to alchemy, while sublimation has its most extensive elaboration in psychoanalysis.

In the case of alchemy, sublation refers to the transformation of base metals (iron, nickel, lead) into the so-called 'noble metals' (silver and gold). These were thought to be perfect; that is, they were substances to which nothing could be added or taken away without violating their purity. They were perfect and therefore complete. The idea of sublation rests upon a central alchemical principle: namely, the transformation of base matter, via refinement, into a 'higher' or an elevated form. Perfect and complete substances were supposed to appear at the climax of the great work.

While formally similar to sublation in that it is concerned with elevation and transformation, sublimation in psychoanalysis is quite different. Psychoanalytic sublimation refers to the ways in which dangerous instinctual drives — drives located in the deepest and most primitive layers of an individual's psyche — are transformed into socially acceptable forms and activities: 'The instinct is said to be sublimated in so far as it is diverted towards a new, non-sexual aim and in so far as its objects are socially valued ones'. (6)

A single instance of a failure to sublimate primitive drives would, of course, be dangerous only for the individual. But a general failure of sublimation would threaten the entire social fabric. Sublimation, to achieve its goal, has to be a collective process with collective ways of dealing with dangerous psychic urges. Freud argued very strongly that if sublimation — the process of psychical transformation — did not take place, the unsublimated elements would pose a threat to civilisation. Sublimation enables individuals to live and be useful in a world where disruption is kept within acceptable limits. Without sublimation, the 'civilised order' would simply not exist. Freud's comment on what is at stake here is especially clear:

> Sublimation of instinct is an especially conspicuous feature of cultural evolution; it is this that makes it possible for the higher mental operations, scientific, artistic, ideological activities to play such an important part in civilised life. (7)

In a general sense, dress is a prime example of the process of sublimation (and sublation). Like sublation, it transforms raw materials into the finished forms that are essential for dress; like sublimation, it has to rework the body into a socially acceptable form, a form that is distinct from the body given to us by nature. As we have seen, the readiness and preparation that is so much a part of dress is to make something that is socially acceptable. So, dress — because of the imperative for it to be a socially approved form — is the place where sublimation happens.

Dress is sublimation in action. It is the outcome of the sublimation of 'base' raw materials and undressed bodies. Sublimation works to ensure the activities of civilisation can proceed without disruption, and dress is the sublimated form that the civilised body takes. Sublimation imparts cohesion, and adhesion, to the various components of dress. It transforms the unfinished into the finished and completes what is incomplete.

It is now possible to line up the *coming into being of dress* with the movement on the staircase and the process of sublimation. In each case, the components of dress are drawn away from Carlyle's unsettling vision of their raw materials and pointed towards the completed individuals who live on the landing, between the two staircases.

Representation

Sublimation is not a mechanical process. It cannot be seen directly nor is it visible through a microscope or any other scientific instrument. Its presence can only be detected through the results it has on the world around it. The only way to study the effects it has on dress is to catch glimpses of those visual depictions, scraps of language and the slight alterations that can happen to our dress. This means that any 'evidence' is always fragmentary and this is because there is no complete picture to uncover.

One difficulty in describing what can happen with the images crucial to the process of sublimation is the words that are usually available to describe what the pictures do. Words such as 'representation', 'depiction', 'image' and 'picture', for example, are almost always followed immediately by 'of''. This carries a sense of a passive receptivity followed by some sort of representation to its viewer. This is not what the images (and the other places of sublimation mentioned) are up to. Sublimation and, as we shall see, unravelling, do not play out solely on empirical dress; the many and varied 'other places' are just as much active participants in the overall process of sublimation as 'real' dress is. They are traces left by sublimation.

Dress and Sublimation

Anyone who has visited a clothing sweatshop would surely have noticed the large mobile baskets into which finished articles of clothing are thrown. As the pile grows, it starts to resemble an undifferentiated mass of material, so much so that it becomes difficult to make out any of the garments' distinctive features. But pick up just one and its identity will be immdiately clear. Its physical characteristics, such as shape, sleeves, colour and pattern orientation, mark it out as something waiting to be introduced to a body. Even at this rudimentary stage it is clear that a body is required to realise the dormant form in the garment. The garment sublimates the flesh and body of the wearer; it absorbs the form of the wearer and transforms it into a *presence*, something that is neither wholly of the body nor the garment.

Because contemporary dress comes into being as a commodity first and a worn garment second, the sublimation of dress in late industrial society takes place almost entirely within the many forms of advertising. What these 'introductions' between body and stuff have in common is that they arrive in the form of an image.3 One way to bring about these introductions is to display the chosen garments in expectation of the body. Some years ago, the owners of a men's outfitter in the town in which I lived in the United Kingdom filled their window with shirts. Each had its arms extended and pinned to one another to hold them fast in the desired shape. It was as if they were miming the moment the bodies were to arrive. This expectation of embodiment imparted excess animation to the shirts. Inert stuff was turned into dancing shirts. (8)

Illustration 5
Advertising Display: Azira shop.
Paris : 2013

The shirts in the window display have taken a few steps along the way to completion. In illustration 5 the shop floor display is heading towards the realms of fashion photography, the fashion show and advertising in general, where all components of dress are present and where they will undergo a form of synchronised sublimation. What is happening in the adverrtising installation that is ill. 5 is the emergence of of 3D figures from out of a flat, 2D world made up of line. This moment of transformation- a moment favoured for window dsiplays and Department store presentations- is the point where it sets out to complete the journey into further realms of ublimation. Further such moments of will take place as the mannequin and its milieu are drawn out of each preceeding stage. (A major moment is the point when the body moves from mannequin to live model.) The bodyThe process of sublimation now approaches the state of completion exhibited by illustration 6. The image, the model and the clothes are the equivalent of the noble elements that resulted from sublation. Like them, we have reached a state of perfection and as this process unfolds a gap opens up between these completed entities and the dress worn on the streets.

Illustration 6
Willy Maywald: Fath Chapeau: Paris:1951

186

The head of the staircase has almost been reached. Before examining the occupants on the landing, one final form of sublimation that contributes to the preparedness of dress must be considered: the work undertaken by the aesthetic. I am using aesthetic here in the sense of 'taking responsibility' for purposefully working the materiality of the stuff and the body. To be material, as stuff and flesh are, means they require attention, and that attention lies in the more restricted modes of the aesthetic, form and style. It is form and style that are responsible for the final ingredient of readiness. With these complete, dress is ready for its materialisation among the people of the landing, or, in a very different form, among the occupants of the strange worlds found on the pages of fashion magazines.

Social approval is crucial to the psychoanalytically inclined version of sublimation for any form of dress to assume material existence. Style and form are equally crucial to producing the sorts of dress that do not violate the codes governing the presentation of the dressed body. The most basic of these is that there is form, while appearance sits within a range of acceptable styles. (9)

Freud's ideas about sublimation drew on his wider notions of the human psyche. Our minds are neither an arena where instinct is allowed free expression nor a place where reason can obliterate our more primitive urges. The psychoanalytically influenced dress scholar J. C. Flugel formulated an approach to dress that he called 'a compromise-formation'. (10) He argues that dress is a compromise that ceaselessly negotiates a balance between the force of the bodily instincts and the demands of sublimated social order. Style and form in dress are that compromise. They are the source of that readiness that is crucial to the discussion of dress.

Sublimation exists because dress does not grow on trees. Its materials and flesh have to be drawn out of nature to become part of our world, the world we call culture. Through the meeting (sublimation) of these two parts, a dressed body emerges that has both social and cultural significance.

It is something close to the provision of an ontological foundation — a 'what-they-are'. Dress is not a wholly utilitarian object, the function and therefore the form of which can be easily predicted. Recall the notion of 'potential', mentioned earlier in the discussion of the dress object: it is open-ended, capable of infinite forms, as it takes its place in our communal activities.

The Landing

Fantastic grow the evening gowns.
W. H. Auden, 'The Fall of Rome'

If we now turn to the people between staircases, to those on the landing, what sorts of dress can we expect them to be wearing? Sublimation and aesthetic compromise will ensure most forms of dress are socially approved and will find a place in the wearer's daily life. However, sublimation is not wholly successful in calming the great variety of dress forms that present themselves. If it were, our social life would resemble a becalmed duck pond. Despite their apparent cohesion and completion, many forms of dress are not as stable as they appear at first sight. Together with those wearing socially approved dress, individuals and groups can also be found that fail, flout and evade the ethos that binds together the sorts of dress worn by the folk on the landing. As Freud indicated, evasion of the final 'work' of sublimation can be an indication of discontent with civilisation as a whole. (11) Cases such as these might be described as *under-sublimated*. Failure to reach a certain degree of sublimation can attract many sorts of denigrating labels, such as slob, scruff, etc.4 Just as in our world of worn dress, on the landing certain individuals will mingle with the crowd in attire that falls far short of the accepted standard.

There are other creatures on the landing, but for the most part they are not made of flesh and blood like everybody else. Like us, those on the landing will see images of people with arms, legs and indeed all the basic elements of the human anatomy. But with their beauty, their dress and the worlds they appear to inhabit, they could almost be a different species. These people, and their dress, seem to be pursuing ideals that lie far beyond the reality of mundane attire. *Over-sublimation* has driven these creatures past the worldly reality in which the rest of us live. What they are wearing is the untrammelled realisation of dress forms. It is the realisation of both formal and aesthetic ideals that make this realm of high fashion something approaching the sublime. It is the place where a full realisation of dress can happen, and this ideal completion means that it can only eventuate in images or in events and places that are close to the principles of imaging. This is why they can only appear as an image among the crowd on the landing.

We are now at the head of the Rowlandson staircase and can begin to explore what lies in store for the inhabitants of the landing.

Desublimation

> The fact that the transcending truths of the fine arts, the aesthetics of life and thought, were accessible only to the few wealthy and educated was the fault of a repressive society. But this fault is not corrected by paperbacks, general education, long playing records and the abolition of formal dress in the theatre and concert hall... No misunderstanding: as far as they go, paperbacks, general education and long playing records are truly a blessing.
>
> Herbert Marcuse, *One Dimensional Man*

Compared to sublimation, desublimation, used here to designate the unravelling of dress, is almost invisible. There is no entry for it in the *New*

Shorter Oxford English Dictionary, nor is it part of alchemical vocabulary as a companion to sublate. It is also absent from where one would think it most likely found: in the discourse of psychoanalysis but there is no sign of it alongside its conceptual sibling, sublimation. (12)

Only one reference is consistently given for desublimation, and that is *One Dimensional Man*, by Frankfurt School philosopher Herbert Marcuse. Even here, Marcuse always couples 'desublimation' with 'repressive' and it is the idea of 'repressive desublimation' that he explores in his book. Put simply, what he tries to explain, via the idea of repressive desublimation, is why, in advanced capitalist societies, it is possible to maintain social control through the liberalisation of the forms and structures of daily life. It is this coupling of social control with an apparent easing of social and cultural regulation that he calls repressive desublimation. Marcuse argues that repressive desublimation is able to reorder great swathes of everyday life in such a way that individuals feel they are living more authentic lives. By relaxing and replacing external regulation with internal (self) control the individual does the controlling for and of him- or herself. Social control is effective because it no longer feels oppressive.

Marcuse thought that repressive desublimation was at work in areas quite separate from the pedestrian routines of daily life. Freud had argued that one of the consequences of sublimation was the creation of a sphere above and beyond the realm of communal acquiescence. This was the place of the sublime, where art, spirituality, utopian imagery, religion, music and dance were redolent of perfection, transcendence and fulfilment. As Freud describes it these are ' the ideals that man has formed, his conceptions of the perfection possible in an individual, in a people, in humanity as a whole, and the demands he makes on the basis of these conceptions'. (12) It is these sublime images that stood in the way of installing the one-dimensional society that is a world bereft of any kind of transcendence.

Revising Desublimation

As powerful as Marcuse's conception of repressive desublimation is, it really needs revising so as to register the particularities of dress. To begin with, 'desublimation' needs to prised away from 'repressive' to allow it to perform other than as an agent of social control. It is not always political, or not in the sense of engaging with broad social distributions of power.

Marcuse invariably described repressive desublimation as something global in reach and political in intent. This *intention* was to affect change wherever and whenever a suitable relaxation in forms of social life presented themselves. Desublimation as it will be used in relation to dress engages with those forms of power manifest at a small scale. At this level, it is often difficult to discern whether the features presented by dress have a political purpose, or not. There is simply no way of identifying the political trajectory of much of the changes that happen with dress. Even Marcuse seems to encounter difficulty in deciding whether long-playing records and paperback books are politically authentic.

One example may help clarify the political ambiguity in the idea of repressive desublimation. Sydney is famous for the string of beaches that stretch the length of the city foreshore. Each beach has its own particular history of how the local population struggled to overturn the regulations through which councils tried to control how the beaches were to be used. Councils regulated when beaches would be open to bathers; they determined who was permitted access (the sexes were often kept separate); and they controlled even what style of swimming costume had to be worn. In 1907, Waverly Shire Council passed a new ordinance requiring a 'skirt-like tunic' be worn by male bathers.' This compulsory bathing costume for men soon became an object of ridicule for local bathers.

> On the morning of Sunday 20 October [1907], thousands of surf bathing enthusiasts poured onto the sands of Bondi, Manly, and Coogee beaches in various types of feminine dress enacting a humorous mockery of the proposed regulations... The support that the protests gained from both the general public and the media proved the end for the Waverly council's costume proposal; the tunic/skirt ordinance was not included in the beach ordinances promulgated in the following months. (13)

Whether these events were a cunning plan on the part of Waverly Shire Council to retreat in order to keep control of the situation or whether they were an authentic piece of popular dress liberation, it is difficult to know where the politics in all this lies.

Marcuse describes repressive desublimation as if its actions were guided by a controlling intention. While there are many cases of intentional and repressive ordinances to control dress, examples of global desublimation with the intention to lift dress restrictions seem to be rare. Desublimation is more likely found in encounters that are small in scale that lack intention and that do not rest on an identifiable agency of any kind. This is because desublimation, unlike sublimation, does not result from a single unravelling force. Again unlike sublimation, which, despite its many detours, moves towards the light of completion and acceptance, desublimation has no such singular aim; so it can and does emerge from the accidental. Such slips of one's dress will often reveal what would normally be hidden, what sublimation has worked hard to conceal. Rowlandson's staircase is a perfect picture of multiple accidents creating a grand scene of collective desublimation.

Dress and Desublimation

The ways in which desublimation works to unravel dress are too many to fully enumerate here, let alone consider in any detail. What follows is an examination of just four types of dress and desublimation in action. In the first — covered in the section 'The Ill-fitting Male' — desublimation appears to take place with little or no concern for context. Indeed, the actions performed by the wearer are themselves the context of the wearer's aim. In other instances context is everything, as will be seen in 'Grammar School'. The explosive unravelling that occurs is a long way from the common characterisation of unravelling as a benign process in the service of liberation. In 'The Elderly and Desublimation' I pursue the theme laid out earlier in the section 'Representation', namely that sublimation and unravelling can happen at a considerable distance from empirical dress. In this example, I follow the way in which desublimation of dress forms an important part of representing the elderly by means of empirical detail and imaginary circumstance. The final example, 'Taunting Fashion', looks at why and how high fashion has been ridiculed using caricature as a vehicle of desublimation.

The Ill-fitting Male

He tried to kiss his mother, but she fended him off and pulled at his clothes, straightening and arranging them with savage little tugs.
Nathanael West, *Day of the Locust*

You will recall that one of the aims of sublimation in creating dress is to produce a degree of coherence between the body of the wearer and the stuff worn. Coherence does not simply mean a set of well-made clothes. It refers to the success in realising the overall form of the ensemble, no matter how eccentric it may be. This coherence is often referred to as the 'fit', which denotes the physical relationship between the wearer and what they are wearing. In fashion photographs, and indeed in many other sorts of dress advertising, the fit between the various parts of dress is usually at its most complete. One of the things the fashion photograph can do is show a complete 'fit', no matter the nature of scene unfolding in the picture. But in contexts such as the everyday, it is inevitable that dress will start to lose its coherence. Movement may reveal that the outfit is no longer a seamless whole but made up of segments, and segments that can have a degree of independence from one another. The movement of segments is a sort of desublimation, coherence undermined by the independent existence of each of the various parts. There is a shift from dress completeness to a state of 'ill-fittedness'. Indications of this can be detected in the adjustments made to restore the garments (and the body) to their proper fit. This drift from a good fit is as much an effect of the body as it is the garments. For male dress — there are different but equivalent points for women and their dress — the adjustments (that is, the rolling back of desublimation) entail a set of manual actions. For example, fixing the area around the waist where a disjunction can occur between trousers and shirt; tucking one's shirt into one's trousers, both front and back; hitching up one's trousers to ensure a smooth transition from trousers to shirt; frequently adjusting the tie to bring it into proper alignment with the collar; and if a waistcoat is worn, pulling it down to produce a smooth surface. With a jacket there may be constant unbuttoning and buttoning, according to the circumstance the wearer finds himself in; he must decide where and when sublimation is appropriate and where and when a 'relaxed' style is appropriate. If there is ambiguity, a confused buttoning and unbuttoning can result.

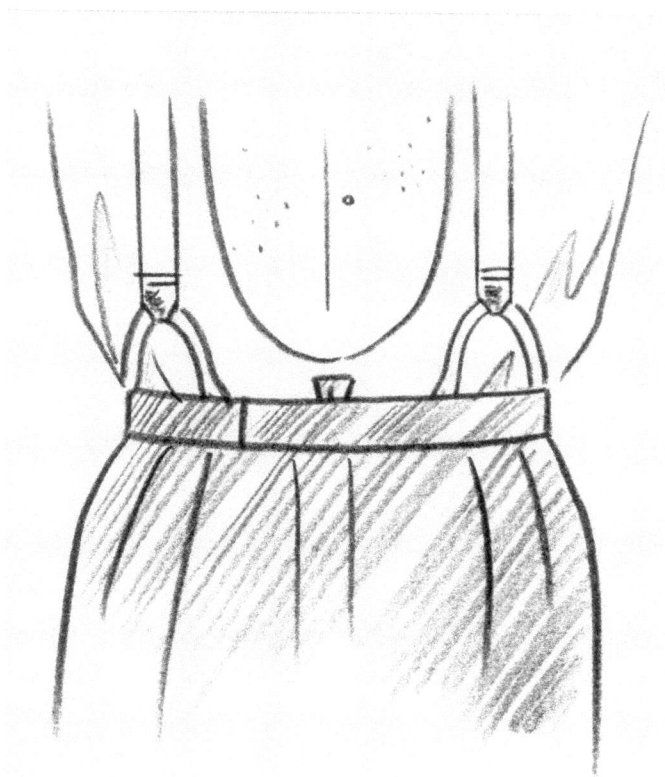

A PROPERLY MADE DINNER SHIRT HAS A
TAB THAT FASTENS TO THE TROUSERS
TO KEEP IT FROM PULLING UP.

Illustration 7
(Anti-desublimation device)
America: 1930's

In casual clothing, the concertinaing of one's trousers at the back of, usually boots has the effect of drawing into question the coherence of the remainder of the wearers dress. For the most part, the wearer is unaware of the wardrobe malfunction and the refusal of their dress to maintain some degree of completion can be comical, as well as embarrassing. One small detail of desublimation — of the ill fitting — can call the whole disposition of one's dress into question. Adjustments are made in the hope of restoring dress to its 'proper' configuration — to its sublimated and complete condition. Dress is in need of constant physical adjustment to restore to it something of the perfection of its initial fit.

Grammar School

In the early 1960s, I attended an all boys grammar school in the south of England. Grammar schools were the elite schools in the state education system and entry depended how one performed in an examination sat at the age of 11. My school was paired with a nearby grammar school for girls, and there were many occasions on which the two schools got together for events such as dances, drama and visits to local historical sites. During one such occasion, one girl had the misfortune of her petticoat becoming visible below the hemline of her skirt. The effect of this very minor display (no more than a couple of inches) on a number of the boys was, even at this distance, frightening. They began to taunt her with some very nasty insults, many of which were crude slurs on her sexual modesty. It wasn't long before she burst into tears and fled the scene.

Not all 'unveilings' brought about by desublimation are benign. When the restraints holding the tribes of Europe from one another's throats evaporated in the 20th century, the resulting slaughterhouse of war makes Freud's concern with the dangers posed by 'unsublimated' elements of the psyche into something more than shallow conservatism. In the case described above, the appearance of the young girl's petticoat precipitated an outbreak of pack cruelty. Why? We need to note that in the United Kingdom, in the 1950s and early 60s, sublimation had ensured that female dress was completely 'exterior'. Nothing beneath what was visible could be seen, nor should be seen. Most tellingly, it was the responsibility of women to maintain the expected level of dress sublimation. This would mean the 'problem' lay with the appearance of the girl's petticoat, a garment that had not undergone sublimation. Following such logic, women's underwear was inherently dangerous. After all wasn't it being kept out of sight because its appearance would be 'improper'? Perhaps this is a variation on the age-old fear of the danger women can inflict on men. ('Cover up or you will inflame men's desires. We can't be held responsible for what we might do. It is not our fault.') But more is dragged into the light and set in motion than an 'indifferent' garment.6 Because the boys glimpsed a couple of inches of female underwear, they were granted permission to act with exceeding cruelty and to launch insults loaded with sexual disgust. The minor and accidental unravelling of the young girl's dress was swept up by a more general and psychic aggression. This desublimation released the boys' sexual contempt, not the sexual ravages caused by the 'potent' garments worn by a young girl.

The Elderly and Desublimation

Do comfy shoes mean we have to sacrifice style?
Guardian. 2014

It is probably impossible to determine when and where the elderly living in richer countries in the West began to coalesce into a subculture, become the object of consumer designs and acquire a distinctive wardrobe. But the increased life expectancy of these populations has given rise to the 'filling in' of the time between retirement and death. If representations of post-work males are anything to go by, the favoured forms of dress are 'relaxed' and 'casual'. There is the Lycra-clad pensioner about to join a marathon and the horror version of aged existence, where the wearer is marooned in a nursing home awaiting death. I am here concerned not with a straightforward account of 'empirical' reality, but rather where the wardrobe of the elderly male sits in the collective imaginary

In the overall scheme of things, the place occupied by the elderly is one that foremost indicates these individuals are no longer full-time participants in the life of their society. They may struggle against their diminished status in the form of frenetic physical activity or else identify with the ethos of compulsory cheerfulness that pervades representations of the elderly. As far as the collective imaginary is concerned, the elderly have relinquished the world of work and everything that goes with it. This means they don't just find themselves in a place of non-work; they are now occupants of a place that is, in many ways, its opposite. It is a place of leisure, or at least a place of profound inactivity.

In comparing the dress favoured for life in an 'elderly' condition with that of worldly work, the former might be considered a radically desublimated wardrobe; the garments of the worker exhibit a much higher level of sublimation. Shirts, ties, suits and lace-up shoes and a high level of visible maintenance, comprise the wardrobe relinquished after leaving worldly work, as they have become inappropriate for situations the elderly are likely to find themselves in. Many of these garments are thought unsuitable because of the need to master a number of tricky dress adjustments. The rationale underpinning elderly dress — and, by implication, bodies — is that practical (useful and comfortable) garments are required rather than those of the worker. The trainers, the tracksuits, the T-shirts, the zips, the cardigans and the Velcro all comprise an imaginary sartorial universe that enfolds the elderly male wearer in usefulness and comfort. The garments make no demands on the bodies of the wearers, which are in a permanent leisure mode. Under the banner of use and comfort, these forms of dress might seem devoid of sartorial rhetoric, but their appearance speaks of a controlled retreat into desublimation.

The dress of the elderly and the world in which the elderly live comprise a place where desublimation rules. For workers, the casual wear they adopt in times of leisure can be discarded when they return to their labours. But what the elderly wears cannot be desublimated any further. The position that the elderly occupy is point zero and from the viewpoint of the world of work, the elderly cannot relax any further. The world of the elderly is in a permanent state of desublimation, and there is a special wardrobe waiting for us all if we are ever drawn towards a final relaxation:

Taunting Fashion

You will recall that an important part of the work undertaken by Marcuse's repressive-desublimation is to undermine the realm of the sublime. What he had in mind was the dilution of sublime content found in such areas as music, architecture, art, utopian social movements and religion. This eating away at the sublime was intended to dissolve what Marcuse called the *promesse de bonheur,* those depictions of a world no longer subject to misery, war, disease and alienation. If the one-dimensional society predicted by Marcuse should have come into being, the realm of the sublime would have disappeared, or at least been seriously undermined. So too would have vanished the invidious comparison between what is and what could be. But this is not quite what happened.

We saw that among the crowd on the landing dressed in daily attire is a species of dress whose sublimation had been pursued so intensely that it could only fully materialise in the form of an image or a word. This is the realm of high fashion, a type of dress whose formal ideals are stretched to their limits and throw up kinds of dress never intended to occupy a place in daily wear. It is this impracticality that places them above the general populace. In many ways the attitude towards this elevated realm, which is the highest of high fashion, is similar to the more obvious manifestations of the sublime. The difference in this instance is that high fashion occupies an elevated position within a commodity universe, where previously it (the sublime) had been the place occupied by the gods. Veneration there certainly is, but its opposite can also be found. There is, and has been, a will to desecrate the very forms of high fashion dress through acts of visual negation, which are at the same time aggressive acts of desublimation.

In its modern sense, fashion (in late-18th-century Europe onwards) has always been accompanied by a parallel discourse made up of caricatures, the aim of which is to pillory and pour scorn on the sorts of dress worn by fashionable elites. How is this derision achieved?

Illustration 8;
George Cruikshank: Monstrosities 1822

Caricature works by taking the materials of an 'original' — this can be a specific set of garments or the bodily attitudes demanded by fashionable deportment — and reworking them using graphic techniques of exaggeration, simplification and stylisation. Caricatures are a mix of mimesis and distortion, for a caricature needs to retain enough of the original for the element of distortion (which is the element of desublimation) to be appreciated by the viewer. Caricature is an ethical genre that works to reveal the truth of fashion by way of ridicule. (14)

Caricature's first action of 'fashion baiting' is to undermine the social elevation enjoyed by high fashion. The images that ridicule the fashionable realm are worldly images, images that transform the dressers into earthbound fools. This is done by selecting a single fashionable element and through exaggeration inverting the relation between the wearer and what is worn (the wearer is worn by their dress rather than the other way round). The logic seems to be that if the fashionable are brought down to our level they will be revealed as idiots rather than the angels they aspire to be. The desublimation of caricature can reveal what had been hidden by the transformations dressed by sublimation. Caricatures of the kind we have been discussing here work to unravel the sublimities of fashion.

Conclusion

Before bringing this discussion of dress and desublimation to a close, I want to pay one last visit to Carlyle's vision of the raw materials out of which our clothes are made — the place where they begin, but also the place where they could also end. Carlyle speaks of this sartorial graveyard when he draws attention to the clothes he himself is wearing, observing that they will eventually 'rot on me'. This is followed by an extraordinary description of how this will come about:

Day after day, I must thatch myself anew; day after day, this despicable thatch must lose some film of its thickness; some film of it, frayed away by tear and wear, must be brushed off into the Ashpit... Till by degrees the whole has been brushed thither, and I, the dust-making, patent Rag-grinder, get new material to grind down. (15)

Carlyle's vision of the end of clothing (not dress) is one of material degradation brought about by 'tear and wear'. Clothes, because they are made of physical materials, are subject to a constant decay that results from such 'tear and wear'. This is the price paid for physical embodiment. It is as if all the garments, together with their raw materials, are heading for a shared condition of dust and a common vanishing point. We are all similarly subject to this law of decomposition.

While desublimation flirts with 'tear and wear' in the shape of distressed garments, and dishevelled looks it has little in common with Carlyle's material disintegration.

It is not primarily concerned with decay, but rather with undoing what sublimation has put in place. Without sublimation it would not exist. This 'undoing' or unravelling can, as we have seen, take a playful form or a dangerous form. We have also seen that desublimation is not just about stuff. Dress comes into being when stuff and flesh (the body) complete one another. Bodies, too, can undergo desublimation and pass through a number of undressed states, or with what becomes of our bodies, as we grow older. To be told that one is not properly or fully dressed is just as much an affair of the body as it is the shortcomings of what one is wearing. Sublimation is, above all else, concerned with assembly — with the bringing into being of dress or with introducing stuff to flesh. Desublimation, in one of its manifestations, brings about a disarticulation of the body from the stuff of dress: ill-fitting clothes or the 'emergency clothing' that accompanies natural disasters, such as the clothing worn by the children in Grozny.

Sublimation has a direction (just one), which arises from the requirement of assembly, putting together. (The staircase is moving upwards.) The process of putting together is governed by a 'correct' sequence and is not a collection of arbitrary events. In other words, the effects of sublimation are cumulative. This is not the case with desublimation, where there are no regular steps downwards, nor are they united by a single downward direction. Desublimation of dress is not unified. It is not singular, nor is it cumulative. It is all over the place.

Notes

(1) Scott Hughes Myerly, from whose book this illustration comes, observes that 'In 1829 the Duke of Wellington was blown off his horse by a gust of wind while wearing this huge cap and swan's feather at a London review'. Myerly, British Military Spectacle: From the Napoleonic Wars Through the Crimea, Harvard University Press, Cambridge, Ma. 1996,

(3) Thomas Carlyle, Sartor Resartus, University of California, Oakland, Ca., 2000 [orig. 1833–34], p. 44.

(4) From here on, for the sake of some degree of variety, I will alternate naming the material dimension of dress as 'stuff', 'clothes' or 'garments'. The New Shorter Oxford Dictionary gives one meanings of stuff as: 'material for making garments'.

(5) The conception of the object presented here is greatly influenced by French thinker Roger Caillois: 'the utilitarian role of an object never completely justifies its form, or to put it another way... the object always exceeds its instrumentality'. Caillois, The Necessity of Mind, Lapis Press, Venice, Ca., 1990, p. 6.

(6) Jean Laplanche and Jean-Bertrand Pontalis, The Language of Psychoanalysis, Karnac Books, London, 1988, p. 431. See also Charles Rycroft, A Critical Dictionary of Psychoanalysis, Penguin, 1968, pp. 159–60.

(7) Sigmund Freud, 'Civilisation and Its Discontents', in Civilisation, War and Death, The Hogarth Press, London, 1968, pp. 42–3.

(8) This is not a strictly accurate description of the stages that make up the sublimation of the shirts. Between the indiscriminate jumble in the sweatshop baskets and the animated shirts in the shop window, is the almost universal practice of boxing the shirts in such a way as to display the shirt with the collar and buttons front on. This arrangement is the first way of presenting the shirt to the customer. It could be that this is just a pleasing, abstract arrangement or, as seems more likely, the presentation of the shirt at the moment of its first encounter with a body, albeit with one yet to fully arrive. There is in these shirts a glimmer of the wearer-to-be's body .

(9) George Bataille examined the manner in which a lack of form- the informe- was capable of inducing disgust, even panic, in an observer. Form becomes a necessary organising principle for all socially acceptable products. See, Bataille, 'Formless', in *Visions of Excess: Selected Writings, 1927-1939*, University of Minnesota Press, 1985, p. 31.

(10) See J. C. Flugel, *The Psychology of Clothes*, The Hogarth Press, London, 1930, p.22.

(11) Sigmund Freud, 'Civilisation and its Discontents', in *Civilisation, War and Death*, Hogarth Press, 1968, p. 4.

(12) There is no sign of it neither in Charles Rycroft, *A Critical Dictionary of Psychoanalysis*, Penguin, Harmondsworth, 1972 nor in Laplanche and Pontalis, *The Language of Psychoanalysis*, Karnac Books, London, 1988.

(13) en.wikipedia.org/wiki/ 1907_Sydney_bathing_cosgtume: accessed 29 May 2014-07-28 also see Ian Warden, 'Men in Skirts: a decidedly grotesque pageant'. *National Library of Australia News*, vol.6 no 2 ,pp 58-60.

(14) See Peter McNeil, 'Fashion and the Eighteenth-Century satirical print', in Riello and McNeil, *The Fashion History Reader: Global, Perspectives*, Routledge, 2010.

(15) Carlyle, *Sartor Resartus*, p. 44.

Bibliography

Barber, E. W., *Women's Work: The First 20,000 Years: Women, Cloth and Society in Early Times,* 1994.

Barthes, Roland, *The Fashion System*, New York, Hill & Wang, 1983.

Barthes, Roland, *The Language of Fashion*, Berg, 2006.

Bataille, Georges, *Visions of Excess: Selected Writings 1927-1939*, University if Minnesota Press, 1985.

Bataille, Georges, *Theory of Religion*, Zone Books, New York, 1992.

Baudelaire, Charles, *Baudelaire: Selected Writings on Art and Artists*, trans. P. Charvet, London, 1972.

Baudrillard, Jean, 'Design and Environment', in For *a Critique of the Political Economy of the Sign*, St. Louis, 1981.

Beaton, Cecil, *The Face of Fashion*, London, 1954.

Benjamin, Walter, *Charles Baudelaire: A Lyric Poet in the Era of High Capitalism*, New Left Books, London, 1973.

Benjamin, Walter, *The Arcades Project*, trans. Howard Eiland and Kevin McLaughlin, The Belknap Press of Harvard University Press, 1999.

Benson E. and J. Esten, *Unmentionables: A Brief history of Underwear*, New York, Simon and Schuster, 1996.

Berry, Andrew, (ed), *Infinite Tropics: An Alfred Russel Wallace Anthology*, Verso, 2002.

The Bible

Briggs, Asa, 'Hats, Caps and Bonnets', in *Victorian Things*, Chicago: University of Chicago Press, 1989.

Brumett, B, *The Rhetoric of Machine Aesthetics*, Greenwood Publishing Group, 1999.

Buck-Morss, Susan, 'Redeeming Mass Culture for the Revolution', *New German Critique*, no. 29, Spring/Summer 1983.

Buck-Morss, Susan, *The Dialectics of Seeing: Walter Benjamin and the Arcades*

Project, MIT Press, 1990

Burman, B, and M. Leverton, 'The Men's Dress Reform Party 1929-1937', in *Costume*, No. 21, 1987.

Burman, Barbara, 'Better and Brighter Clothes: The Men's Dress Reform Party, 1929 – 1940', in *Journal of Design History*, 8 (4), 1995.

Caillois, Roger, *The Necessity of Mind*, Lapis Press, Venice Ca., 1990.

Calverton, V.F. (ed.) *The Making of Man: an Outline of Anthropology*, The Modern Library, 1931.

Carlyle, Thomas, *Sartor Resartus*, University of California Press, 2000.

Carter, Michael, *Fashion Classics from Carlyle to Barthes*, Berg, Oxford, 2003.

De Castelbajac, Kate, *The Face of the Century: 100 Years of Makeup and Style*, Thames and Hudson, London, 1995.

Chapman, Anne, 'The Great Ceremonies of the Selk'nam and the Yamana' in McEwan, Colin, Borrero, Luis A. and Prieto, Alfredo in McEwan, Borrero, and Alfredo (eds) *Patagonia: Natural History, Prehistory and Ethnography at the Uttermost End of the Earth*, British Museum Press, 1997.

Clark, Fiona, *Hats*, London: Anchor Press, 1982.

Cohn, Nik, *Today There are no Gentlemen*, Weidenfield and Nicholson, London, 1971.

Cole, Shaun, *The History of Men's Underwear*, New York, Parkstone International, 2010.

Coleridge, S.T., *Biographia Literaria*, in The Major Works, Oxford, 1985.

Corfield, P. J., 'Dress for Deference and Dissent: Hats and the Decline of Hat Honour', in *Costume*, 1989.

Corson, Richard, *Fashions in Makeup: From Ancient Rome to Modern Times*, London, 1972.

Craik, Jennifer, ' I Must Put My Face On": Making Up the Body and Marking Out the Feminine', in *Cultural Studies*: 1.3, 1989

Cunnington, C. Willett and Phillis, *The History of Underclothes*, London, Michael Joseph, 1951.

Darwin, Charles, *The Origin of Species*, Penguin, 1985.

Darwin, Charles, *The Descent of Man*, Penguin, 2004.

De Lillo, Don, *White Noise*, Picador, London, 2011.

Derrida, Jacques, 'The Parergon', in *The Truth in Painting*, Chicago: Chicago University Press, 1987.

Desmond, Adrian and James Moore, *Darwin*, London, 1991.

Diller, Elizabeth and Ricardo Scofidio, *Bad Press: Dissident Ironing, 1993-98*: www.youtube.com/watch?v=0zz4Kpqrh9M

Douglas, Mary, *Purity and Danger: An Analysis of Concepts of Pollution and Taboo*, Harmondsworth, I 966.

Dunbar, Robin, Chris Knight, and Camilla Power, *The Evolution of Culture*, Rutgers U. P. 2003.

Dutt, Robin, 'Men's Formal Wear', in Valerie Steele (ed.), *The Berg Companion to Fashion*, Berg, Oxford, 2000.

Entwistle, Joanne, *The Fashioned Body*, Polity Press, 2000.

Ewing, Elizabeth, *History of Twentieth Century Fashion*, London: Batsford, 3rd edn 1986.

Fletcher, Angus, *Allegory: the Theory of a Symbolic Mode*, Ithaca, 1964.

Flugel, J. C. 'Sex Differences in Dress', in *World League for Sexual Reform: Proceedings*, K. Paul, Trench, Trubner, London, 1930.

Flugel, J.C., The Psychology of Clothes, Hogarth Press, 1971 edition.

Flusser, Alan, *Dressing the Man: Mastering the Art of Permanent Fashion*, Harper Collins, New York, 2001.

Focillon, Henri, *The Life of Forms in Art*, New York: Zone Books, 1992.

Freud, Sigmund, *Civilisation, War and Death*, The Hogarth Press, London, 1968.

Gernsheim, Alison, *Fashion and Reality*, London: Faber & Faber 1963.

Gero, Joan M. and Margaret W. Conkey, *Engendering Archaeology: Women and*

Prehistory, Blackwell, 1991.

Gill, Alison and Abby Mellick Lopes, 'On Wearing: A Critical Framework for Valuing Design's Already Made', in *Design and Culture*, vol. 3, issue 3, 2011.

Gilligan, Ian, 'Clothing and modern human behaviour: prehistoric Tasmania as a case study', in *Archaeology in Oceania*, December 2007.

Gombrich, Ernst, *Sense of Order: a Study in the Psychology of Decorative Art*, Oxford: Phaidon, 1984.

Harvey, J.R., *Men in Black*, Reaktion Books, London, 1995.

Haynes, Alan, 'Murderous Millinery', *History Today*, vol. 33, Issue 7, 1983.

Hegel, G.W.F., *Introductory Lectures on Aesthetics*, ed. Michael Inwood, Penguin, 1993.

Hollander, Anne, *Sex and Suits: the evolution of modern dress*, Kodansha International, New York, 1994.

Hollander, Anne, 'Wear and Tear', in *London Review of Books*, Vol. 19, No. 3, 6 February 1997.

Ingold, T. (ed), *What is an Animal?* Unwin Hyman, 1988.

Jameson, Frederic, 'Introduction/Prospectives to Reconsider the Relationship of Marxism to Utopian Thought', in *Minnesota Review*, No. 6, spring, 1976.

Kirkham, Pat. (ed.), *The Gendered Object*, Manchester University Press, 1996.

Laplanche, J. and J.B. Pontalis, *The Language of Psychoanalysis*, Karnac Books, 1988.

Laver, James, *Taste and Fashion: From the French Revolution to the Present Day*, London: G.G. Harrap & Co. Ltd, 1945.

Lewis-Williams, David, *The Mind in the Cave*, Thames and Hudson, 2002.

MacCallum, W.G. and W.H. Welch, *William Stewart Halstead, Surgeon*, Johns Hopkins Press, Baltimore, 1930

Mantel, Hilary, *A Place of Greater Safety*, Fourth Estate, London, 1992.

Marcuse, Herbert, *One Dimensional Man*, Abacus, London, 1968.

Martin, Richard and Harold Koda, *Splash: A History of Swimwear*, New York, Rizzoli, 1990.

Mark, Karl, *The Eighteenth Brumaire of Louis Napoleon*, Lawrence and Wishart, London, 1987.

McInerney, Jay, et al., *Dressed to Kill: James Bond the Suited Hero*, Paris, Flammarion, 1996.

McNeil, Peter, 'Fashion and the Eighteenth-Century satirical print', in Riello and McNeil, *The Fashion History Reader: Global, Perspectives*, Routledge, 2010.

Myerly, Scott Hughes, *British Military Spectacle: From the Napoleonic Wars Through the Crimea*, Harvard University Press, Cambridge, and Ma. 1996.

Noever, P. (ed) *The Future is Our Only Goal: Aleksandr M. Rodchenko*, Varvara F. Stepanova. Noever, Prestel, New York, 1991.

Portmann, Adolf, *Animal Forms and Patterns: A Study of the Appearance of Animals*, Faber, London, 1952.

Ribeiro, Aileen, 'Utopian Dress', in *Chic Thrills: A Fashion Reader*, eds. Juliet Ash and Elizabeth Wilson, London, 1992.

Rycroft, Charles, *A Critical Dictionary of Psychoanalysis*, Penguin, 1972.

Sennett, Richard, *The Fall of Public Man*, Cambridge University Press, 1977.

Simmel, Georg, 'The Philosophy of Fashion', in *Simmel on Culture*, Frisby and Featherstone, 1997, Sage, London.

Slotten, Ross A., *The Heretic in Darwin's Court: The Life of Alfred Russel Wallace*, Columbia University Press, 2004.

Sontag, Susan, *Against Interpretation*, New York, 1961.

Sprawson, C., *Haunts of the Black Masseur*, London, Vintage, 1993.

Stocking Jnr, George, *Victorian Anthropology*, New York, Free Press,

1987.

Strathern, Marilyn, 'The Self in Self-Decoration', *Oceania*, 49.4, June 1979.

Swift, Jonathan, *Jonathan Swift: Selected Poems*, Penguin, London, 1993.

Trinkaus, Erik and Pat Shipman, *The Neanderthals: Changing the Image of Mankind*, Pimlico, London, 1994.

Tseelon, Efra, 'Is Identity a Useful Tool?', in *Critical Studies in Fashion and Beauty*, vol. 1, no. 2, Leeds, 2010.

Tylor, Sir E.B., *Anthropology*, 2 vols. London, Watts & Co, 1930. London, 1930.

Veblen, Thorstein, *The Theory of the Leisure Class*, New York, Penguin, 1994.

Warden, Ian, 'Men in Skirts: A Decidedly Grotesque Pageant', *National Library of Australia News*, vol.6, no. 2, (2007).

en.wikipedian.org/wiki/1907_Sydney_bathing_costume

Wilcox, Turner, *The Mode in Hats and Headdresses*, New York: Charles Scribners and Sons, 1945.

Wilson, Elizabeth, *Adorned in Dreams*, Virago, London, 1985.

Wilson, Elizabeth, *Bohemians: the Glamorous Outcasts*, Tauris Peake, London, 2000.

Wolfe, Tom, *Kandy-Kolored Tangerine-Flake Streamline Baby*, Farrar, Strauss and Giroux, New York 1965.